# AGE RESTRICTED SALES

# AGE RESTRICTED SALES

## THE LAW IN ENGLAND AND WALES

Second Edition

Tony Allen MSc, DTS, DMS, MCTSI
Managing Director, Under Age Sales Ltd
Former Chief Trading Standards Officer
Former Chair Trading Standards North West, Under Age Sales Strategy Group

Matador
9 Priory Business Park,
Wistow Road, Kibworth Beauchamp,
Leicestershire. LE8 0RX
Tel: (+44) 116 279 2299
Fax: (+44) 116 279 2277
Email: books@troubador.co.uk
Web: www.troubador.co.uk/matador

ISBN 978 1784624 194

British Library Cataloguing in Publication Data.
A catalogue record for this book is available from the British Library.

Typeset in 10pt Calibri by Troubador Publishing Ltd, Leicester, UK
Printed and bound in the UK by TJ International, Padstow, Cornwall

**Matador** is an imprint of Troubador Publishing Ltd

For Oliver and Sophie

## TABLE OF CONTENTS

**CHAPTER ONE**
**INTRODUCTION TO THE LAW OF AGE RESTRICTED GOODS**     **1**

**CHAPTER TWO**
**ALCOHOL**     **11**

**CHAPTER THREE**
**TOBACCO**                                                                  **25**

## CONTENTS                                                                   25

**CHAPTER FOUR**
**KNIVES, OFFENSIVE WEAPONS AND FIREARMS**                                  **37**

## CONTENTS                                                                   37

## CHAPTER FIVE
## LOTTERY AND GAMBLING    53

CONTENTS    53

## CHAPTER SIX
## SOLVENTS, AEROSOL PRODUCTS & PETROLEUM    67

CONTENTS    67

**CHAPTER SEVEN**
**FIREWORKS AND EXPLOSIVES**                                                77

CONTENTS                                                                    77

**CHAPTER EIGHT**
**VIDEOS, DVDS, GAMES AND HARMFUL PUBLICATIONS**                            89

CONTENTS                                                                    89

**CHAPTER NINE**
**OTHER AGE RESTRICTED GOODS AND SERVICES** **109**

CONTENTS

**CHAPTER TEN**
**REASONABLE PRECAUTIONS AND DUE DILIGENCE** **123**

CONTENTS

**CHAPTER ELEVEN**
**POWERS OF LAW ENFORCEMENT OFFICERS**                                **139**

CONTENTS                                                             139

## FOREWORD

This book brings together all of the law, practice, guidance and policies relating to age restricted sales. It is a complex and controversial area of law that affects thousands of retailers, shops, pubs, clubs and organisations. The book is the first time a comprehensive and authoritative account of age restricted sales law has been brought together.

Back in 2005, Tony Allen was instrumental in leading the Trading Standards profession negotiating with the government to prepare an agreed strategy paper between the Chartered Trading Standards Institute and the Home Office on our role in tackling crime and disorder. This included a commitment to take action to prevent harm to children and nuisance caused by young people from access to restricted goods. It is testament to the strategy paper that the commitments made are now seen as a cornerstone of Trading Standards work throughout the UK. Tony has taken his substantial experience and knowledge of age restricted sales law and practice and distilled it into this useful book.

The National Framework for Age Restricted Products and Services published by the government's Better Regulation Delivery Office, together with a code of practice and streamlining of age restrictions are all covered in this new book. It is an essential publication for all Trading Standards Departments, Police, Licensing, Community Safety, Retail Compliance Departments and Solicitors or Barristers specialising in Regulatory Law.

The Chartered Trading Standards Institute is committed to leading our profession to continuous improvement. This book helps to consolidate and clarify key aspects of age restricted sales legislation and I recommend it to the profession and beyond.

Leon Livermore
Chief Executive
Chartered Trading Standards Institute

**PREFACE**

This second edition provides a full update of all of the law, practice, guidance and procedures associated with age restricted products. There are at least 238 age restricted products or services in England and Wales (see the table of age restrictions on page 177). The book is intended for practitioners in this field, such as trading standards officers, licensing officers, police officers, community safety officers, corporate compliance managers and licence holders. The book is supported by a dedicated website (www.underagesales.co.uk) where the latest news, views and changes can be found.

The book aims to provide an authoritative and comprehensive account of all aspects of the law of age restricted sales in England and Wales. Although the law in Scotland and Northern Ireland is similar, it is not identical and this book does not cover those jurisdictions. The book tries to set out the law as it stood at the end of May 2015, but this is a rapidly changing area of law and readers are encouraged to visit the supporting website for the latest changes.

The author wishes to thank John Cassin, John Garforth, Brandon Cook, Christine Heemskerk, Jennifer Allen, Janet Hampson, Lionel Titchener and the staff at Matador for their invaluable assistance with the compilation, review and proof reading of the book.

Finally, the author welcomes suggestions for inclusion or corrections, should there be any, for subsequent editions. Readers are encouraged to submit suggestions via the website.


Tony Allen

## TABLE OF CASES

## TABLE OF STATUTES

## TABLE OF STATUTORY INSTRUMENTS

CHAPTER ONE

# INTRODUCTION TO THE LAW OF AGE RESTRICTED GOODS

## CONTENTS

## Introduction

It is reported that Queen Elizabeth considered two gallons of ale only a proper daily allowance for the eight children who sang in the Chapel Royal at St. James's Palace[1].

Over the course of the 17th and 18th Century, the role of the state evolved to form a social contract, including as protector of the vulnerable and children. By the 19th Century, an aspect of this began to be codified in law as age restrictions.

In 1839[2], the sale of distilled spirits to children under 16 for consumption on the premises was banned in the Metropolitan Police District. Since then, age restrictions have gradually been introduced on a broad array of products considered to be harmful to children, or likely to contribute to nuisance caused by young people. This is a growing list and the legislation is piecemeal, often implemented as a result of specific concern over individual products.

The latest product to be added to the list are nicotine inhaling devices (commonly known as e-cigarettes), but still to come are potential restrictions on sharing information online, such as through social networking sites. A comprehensive list of all 238 products and services that are age restricted in England and Wales can be found on pages 177 to 197.

### 1.2    Age Restricted Products and Services Framework

In November 2011, the Local Better Regulation Office[3] published an agreed set of shared responsibilities and reasonable expectations for young people, parents, businesses, employees and regulators with regard to the supply of age restricted products and services. These principles have clear implications for businesses – to put appropriate controls in place and provide effective staff training – but also to clarify what businesses can expect from regulators in return.

---

[1] Bolland, W.C., *A Manual of Year Book Studies* (1925)
[2] S.43, Metropolitan Police Act 1839
[3] Now the Better Regulation Delivery Office and part of the Department for Business, Innovation and Skills

### 1.2.1   Responsibilities and Expectations of Young People

Responsibilities:

- To have regard to information on the risks associated with age restricted products and services and to take responsibility for their own health and wellbeing
- To be good role models to their peers and to younger children in relation to age restricted products and services
- To show valid proof of age when asked to do so
- Not to use 'fake' proof of age, or proof of age that they are not entitled to use and to be aware that by doing so they may commit a criminal offence
- To be aware of the consequences for themselves if they purchase, attempt to purchase or are found in possession of certain age restricted products
- Not to attempt to buy or access age restricted products or services, recognising that this could result in a criminal offence being committed by the business or member of staff
- Not to use threats or intimidation where access to the sale of an age restricted product or service is refused by a business or member of staff
- Not to ask an adult to purchase alcohol on their behalf and to be aware that if the adult did so they may commit a criminal offence

Reasonable Expectations:

- To be provided with clear information on the reasons for age restrictions that seek to protect young people
- To be challenged to show valid proof of age whenever they attempt to access age restricted products or services
- To have valid proof of age accepted by retailers, service providers, licensed premises and door staff
- To be refused products and services that should not be available to them

### 1.2.2   Responsibilities and Expectations of Parents, Carers and Responsible Adults

Responsibilities:

- To help their children to understand the risks associated with age restricted products and services and the reasons for legal restrictions on access to them
- To be aware of the legal restrictions on access to certain products and services by young people

- To be aware of the influence of their own behaviour on their children's behaviour in relation to age restricted products and services
- To ensure that their children understand that they may commit a criminal offence if they use 'fake' proof of age or proof of age belonging to someone else
- Not to commit a criminal offence by purchasing alcohol on behalf of a young person
- To report any concerns about illicit supplies of age restricted products and services to an enforcement agency
- Not to send their children to purchase age restricted products on their behalf

Reasonable Expectations:

- That clear information should be available on the risks associated with age restricted products and services, and on the legal restrictions
- That retailers and suppliers will comply with age restricted products and services legislation
- That other adults will refuse to purchase alcohol on behalf of young people
- That information should be available on how to report concerns about illegal sales of age restricted products and services to young people
- That regulators and enforcers will deal firmly with businesses that deliberately or persistently allow young people to access age restricted products and services that they are not entitled to access

### 1.2.3   Responsibilities and Expectations of Businesses

Responsibilities:

- To promote a culture where young people always expect to be challenged and to have to show valid proof of age whenever they attempt to access age restricted products or services
- To be clear that they accept PASS cards as proof of age (see section 10.3, *post*), and to be clear what other forms of proof of age they will accept
- To put in place appropriate controls to prevent breaches of age restrictions, and to keep these under review (see chapter ten, *post*)
- To provide effective training to those responsible for implementing the controls
- To support sales staff and others responsible for implementing the controls, so that they feel able to check proof of age and to refuse access to products or services
- To mutually share information with regulators and enforcers on local

problems with age restricted products and services, within the context of collaborative working arrangements

Reasonable Expectations:

- That regulators and enforcers should be accountable and transparent in their approaches
- To have access to clear guidance on legislation
- To receive compliance support from regulators and enforcers that is appropriate to their needs and resources
- That regulators and enforcers will recognise and work in a proportionate manner with a business's compliance arrangements, including through Primary Authority[4], when responding to complaints, intelligence and breaches
- To be informed in writing, in a timely manner, of the outcome of a check on their compliance by test purchase or inspection
- To be treated in a consistent manner by different regulators and enforcers dealing with similar provisions
- An approach to sanctions and penalties that is consistent with the principles set out in the Regulators' Compliance Code (see section 11.7, *post*), including dealing firmly with businesses that deliberately or persistently allow young people to access age restricted products and services that they are not entitled to access

### 1.2.4 Responsibilities and Expectations of Employees and Staff

Responsibilities:

- To recognise the key role that employees and staff play in restricting the access that young people have to age restricted products and services
- To support a culture where young people always expect to be challenged and to have to show valid proof of age whenever they attempt to access age restricted products or services
- To be aware of the law and the age restrictions for the products / services for which they are responsible
- Not to commit an offence in relation to these restrictions
- To follow their employer's instructions on age restricted products and services

---

[4] A Primary Authority is a statutory arrangement between a multi-site business and a single local authority under the Regulatory Enforcement and Sanctions Act 2008

Reasonable Expectations:

- To be safe at work
- To be properly trained on age restricted products and services by their employer (see section 10.4, *post*)
- To be properly supported by their employer and colleagues so that they feel able to refuse access to age restricted products and services
- That information should be available on how to report incidents where threats and/or violence have been used against them in an attempt to access age restricted products or services
- To be dealt with in a fair, reasonable and timely manner by their employer where they breach age restrictions
- That information should be available on how to report concerns about young people's sources of age restricted products and services
- To be dealt with in a proportionate and timely manner by regulators and enforcers where they breach age restrictions
- To be treated in a consistent manner by different regulators and enforcers dealing with similar provisions

### 1.2.5 Responsibilities and Expectations of Enforcers

Responsibilities:

- To be clear about the outcomes that they are working towards, and how their activities will contribute to those outcomes
- To ensure that their compliance and enforcement approach to age restricted products and services legislation is transparent
- To work collaboratively with partner organisations and other regulators and enforcers that have overlapping areas of responsibility, to ensure that the overall approach is consistent and focussed on delivering outcomes
- To take an evidence based approach to determining priority risks to local communities and young people
- To prioritise resource allocation on activities that deliver improved protections for local communities and young people, including working in partnership with businesses and local communities to tackle issues of access to age restricted products and services
- To take a risk-based approach to targeting checks on the compliance of individual businesses, and to ensure that their risk assessment model is transparent
- To be clear and consistent in their message that valid proof of age should always be required where young people seek to access age restricted products or services

- To be clear in their message that PASS cards are the preferred form of proof of age, and to acknowledge that there are other acceptable forms of proof of age (see section 10.3, *post*)
- To respond to complaints, intelligence and breaches in a proportionate manner that recognises the business's compliance arrangements and works with them, including through Primary Authority
- When using particular tactics, to seek the appropriate authorisations or approvals as required by legislation or as set out in a code of practice or procedure[5]
- To communicate to businesses in writing, in a timely manner, the outcome of all checks on compliance by test purchase or inspection
- To share good practice and innovation with other regulators and enforcers
- To have regard to the welfare of test purchasers when carrying out test purchases

Reasonable Expectations:

- That businesses will take a responsible approach to complying with legal requirements in relation to age restricted products and services
- That they will receive co-operation from other public sector organisations that share a responsibility for protecting young people, local communities and animals from the harm associated with age restricted products and services

## 1.3   Simplification of Age Restricted Sales Laws

In 2011, as a part of the government's 'red tape challenge', the Secretary of State for Business, Innovation and Skills announced a review and simplification of age restricted sales laws.

In January 2012, the government announced that it planned to improve rather than scrap the range of age restricted sales legislation. Although many respondents to their consultation exercise called for the piecemeal legislation to be scrapped and replaced with a single piece of legislation, there was no commitment made to do this.

The government have said that they plan to simplify the process for age verification.

---

[5] This refers to certain circumstances where covert surveillance powers are utilised by Trading Standards Officers. Covert surveillance powers for investigating the sale of alcohol and tobacco to children were protected by the Regulation of Investigatory Powers (Directed Surveillance and Covert Human Intelligence Sources) (Amendment) Order 2012.

The Deregulation Act 2015 has removed the age restrictions on liqueur chocolates (see p.5.2.8, *post*).

## 1.4   Age of Majority

All age restricted legislation refers to prohibitions on the sale of the relevant product or service to a child, a young person, a minor or an infant. Unfortunately, there is no uniformity in the application of these terms, with different ages applying to different products. See section 1.5, *post*, for the varying definitions of a 'child', 'young person', etc.

At common law a minor was a person aged under 21 years, but this was reduced to 18 and given statutory force by S.1 of the Family Law Reform Act 1969[6]. Thus, in England and Wales, a person reaches the age of majority on the commencement of the 18th anniversary of their birthday[7]. This is the legal demarcation between childhood and adulthood. The age of majority differs from country to country; it is 16 in Scotland, for instance.

The term 'age of majority' collectively describes the various laws that bestow the status of adulthood and, therefore, the control the person has over their own affairs. However, it is not strictly the description of when a child becomes able to purchase age restricted products. This is, perhaps, better described as the 'age of licence'. This is the age at which the state confers on individuals a licence to buy or use or participate in the activity or product. Often the 'age of majority' coincides with the 'age of licence', however, it might not. For instance, the law permits (or licences) participation in the National Lottery to persons aged 16 or over, but prohibits participation in gambling until they reach the age of 18.

In some cases, the 'age of licence' can be older than the 'age of majority'. For instance, certain types of driving licence are restricted to persons aged over 21.

Both the 'age of majority' and 'age of licence' are fixed legal dates, they are unconnected to the level of mental or physical maturity of the individual. In England and Wales, a person cannot be deemed to reach the 'age of majority' by a process of emancipation (this differs to many other jurisdictions where minors who marry, obtain economic independence, obtain a degree or diploma or join military service can be deemed to have reached an 'age of majority').

---

[6] Family Law Reform Act 1969, c46
[7] *Ibid*, S.9.

The appearance and physical maturity of an individual is irrelevant to the sale of age restricted products to children and young people. In the case of alcohol, one of the available defences to a charge of selling alcohol to a child includes a provision that 'nobody could reasonably have suspected from the individual's appearance' that they were under 18. (Note: this is not the complete defence, see section 2.5 *post*)

Although the 'age of majority' has relevance to certain age restrictions and capacity to contract (see section 9.10, *post*), this book focuses on the criminal sanctions created by statute to protect children from harm and prevent nuisance by young people.

## 1.5    Definitions

### 1.5.1    *Minor*

A minor is defined by S.1 of the Family Law Reform Act 1969 as a person who has not reached the age of majority (see section 1.4, *ante*). The age of majority in England and Wales is the commencement of the 18th anniversary of a person's birth date.

### 1.5.2    *Young Person*

A young person is defined in legislation as a specific range of people. It is not consistent. Section 1 of the Gambling Act 2005 defines a young person as a person aged 16 – 18 years of age, but section 107 of the Children and Young Persons Act 1933 defines a young person as a person aged 14 – 18.

### 1.5.3    *Child*

Similarly to the definition of a young person, a child is defined in specific legislation. Typically, it relates to a person who is not yet a young person. So using the examples in section 1.5.2 above, a child under the Gambling Act 2005 would be under 16, a child under the Children and Young Persons Act 1933 would be under 14.

CHAPTER TWO

# ALCOHOL

## CONTENTS

## 2.1    Introduction

Alcohol is probably the main product that people think of when considering age restricted sales. The rules on under age sales of alcohol stem from 1839[1] and, today, are consolidated into the Licensing Act 2003.

Alcohol means[2] spirits, wine, beer, cider or any other fermented, distilled or spirituous liquor, but does not include:

- Alcohol which is of a strength not exceeding 0.5% by volume at the time of supply
- Perfume
- Flavouring essences (provided they are approved by HM Revenue & Customs)
- Angostura Bitters (a type of flavouring essence)
- Alcohol in medicines or veterinary medicines[3]
- Denatured alcohol (poisonous or unpalatable so as to be undrinkable)
- Methyl alcohol (also known as methanol, wood spirits or naphtha)
- Liqueur confectionary (see section 2.8, post)

## 2.2    Key Legislation

Licensing Act 2003

## 2.3    Summary of Age Restricted Laws relating to Alcohol

- Alcohol must not be sold to a person under the age of 18 years
- Children under 16 years are not permitted in pubs and clubs unless they are accompanied by an adult over the age of 18 years
- A person under the age of 18 years may not buy or attempt to buy alcohol
- A person under the age of 18 years may not consume alcohol in a licensed premises unless it is beer, wine or cider, they are 16 or 17 years, it is served with a table meal and they are supervised by an adult

---

[1] Metropolitan Police Act 1839
[2] Section 191(1) Licensing Act 2003
[3] Inserted by the Veterinary Medicines Regulations 2006 (SI2006:2407)

- A person may not buy alcohol on behalf of a person under the age of 18 years
- All sales of alcohol must be supervised by a person over the age of 18 years (although it is permissible for a person under the age of 18 years to process the transaction)
- It is a defence for the person who sold alcohol to a young person to show that they believed the young person was over 18 and that they had taken steps to verify the persons age, or that no-one could reasonably have suspected the person was under 18
- It is a defence for the shop owner/licence holder (provided they didn't sell the alcohol themselves) to show that they had exercised all due diligence to avoid selling alcohol to children
- All of the above carry an unlimited fine in a Magistrates' Court
- If alcohol is sold to a young person on two or more occasions from the same premises within a three month period, this offence carries an unlimited fine, a suspension of licence or a closure order
- It is an offence to give alcohol to a child under the age of 5 years unless it is under the supervision of a medical practitioner

2.4     Prohibition of Children on Certain Premises

Section 145 of the Licensing Act 2003 prohibits children under the age of 16 years from being on certain premises, unless they are accompanied by an adult over 18 years of age.

By section 145 (1) (a), if a person *knows* that a premises is exclusively or primarily used for the supply of alcohol for consumption on the premises, he will commit an offence if he allows an unaccompanied child to be on the premises at any time when it is open for the supply of alcohol. Section 145 (1) (b) states that it is not necessary for the offender to know if the premises are relevant premises if the unaccompanied child is on the premises between midnight and 5:00am.

This offence can only be committed by the designated premises supervisor, premises licence holder, an officer of a club holding a club premises certificate, the premises user holding a temporary event notice or any person working at the premises in a capacity, whether paid or unpaid, which authorises him to ask the unaccompanied child to leave the premises.

The key point to note here is that the offence of allowing those under 16 onto licensed premises without an accompanying adult is only committed if the premises are relevant premises, which means they are primarily used for the supply of alcohol for consumption on the premises. There is, therefore, a whole range of licensed premises which would not be classed as relevant premises, such as bowling alleys, snooker halls, cinemas and possibly many other multi-purpose venues.

The guidance issued under S.182 of the Licensing Act 2003 also deals with this issue in paragraph 13.43 and 13.44 and confirms the general prohibition against allowing children under 16 who are unaccompanied to be on relevant premises and the additional prohibition between midnight and 5:00am. The guidance goes onto consider the meaning of 'exclusively and primarily' in relation to alcohol and paragraph 13.45 states 'the expression should be given its ordinary and natural meaning in the context of the particular circumstances. It would normally be quite clear that the business being operated at the premises is predominantly the sale and consumption of alcohol'.

What is clear, however, is that licensed premises such as hotels, where the main business will be the provision of accommodation, cinemas, where the main business will be watching the films, and snooker halls, where the main business will be playing snooker, will not be relevant premises and will not therefore be covered by section 145 of the Licensing Act 2003.

Where a person is charged with an offence by reason of his own conduct under this section, it is a defence for him to demonstrate that he believed the child to be over 16 or the accompanying adult to be over 18, and either had asked the individual his age and the evidence provided would have convinced a reasonable person or where nobody could reasonably have suspected from the individual's appearance that he was aged under 16 or, as the case may be, under 18.

Where a person is charged with an offence by reason of the act or default of another, it is a defence for him to demonstrate that he exercised all due diligence to avoid committing it. For more information on reasonable precautions and due diligence, see chapter ten, *post*.

2.5     Sale of Alcohol to Children

Section 146, 147 and 147A of the Licensing Act 2003 prohibit the sale of alcohol to children, allowing alcohol to be supplied to children or persistently selling alcohol to children.

By section 146 (1) a person commits an offence if he sells alcohol to an individual aged under 18 years.

Section 146 (2) and (3) contain a similar offence for supplies taking place under a club premises certificate.

The person making the sale must be a licence holder or the person actually making or authorising the sale[4]. A non-licensed owner of alcohol, where that person (whether an individual, corporate or unincorporated body) owns the premises from which the alcohol was sold and employs the licensee of those premises, cannot make a sale for the purposes of what is now S.146 of the Licensing Act 2003. The *Haringey v Marks & Spencer* case was decided under the old provisions of S.169A of the Licensing Act 1964, which are materially identical to the new S.146. However, what has changed is who can be a 'licence holder' under the new Act. This means that a premises licence holder could be the corporate body that owns the alcohol, in which case, could commit the offence.

The sale does not have to take place in licensed premises, it could be anywhere. However, a sale must take place. Merely offering to sell or giving the alcohol to a child is not sufficient for this offence, instead see the offence of delivering alcohol to a child (S.151 Licensing Act 2003, *post*). For a sale to take place to a child, there must be:

- An offer made by the child (not by any adult accompanying them) to purchase alcohol[5] from the seller
- The seller must accept that offer to purchase the alcohol, and
- There must be an exchange (usually money) in return for the alcohol – this is called 'consideration'

The transaction must be complete. No offence is committed under S.146 (1) until the whole sale is completed, thus the seller can legitimately refuse to accept the offer to purchase the alcohol and avoid the offence. The transaction does not have to be recorded in writing and no receipt is necessary. A verbal agreement will suffice.

The transaction does not have to involve payment in money. It can involve consideration (money's worth) of any kind, including sexual favours. The offence would still be committed if alcohol was supplied to a person under 18 years of age in return for sexual favours instead of cash.

---

[4] *London Borough of Haringey & Anor v Marks & Spencer & Anor* [2004] EWHC 1141 (Admin)
[5] The prosecution are not required to prove by analysis that the product is actually alcohol; magistrates are entitled to draw that inference from its manner of labelling *City of Sunderland Council v Dawson* [2004] EWHC 2796 (Admin)

The child must be under 18 years of age. That is, their certificate of birth must show that they were born less than 18 whole years prior to the date of sale. The time of day they were born is not relevant (i.e. a person born at 10.30pm on 1st January becomes 18 on the 18th anniversary of that day, not at 10.30pm on the 18th anniversary)[6]. Some magistrates' have refused to accept just a certificate of birth as evidence of the age of test purchase volunteers leading many Trading Standards Departments to take witness statements from a parent proving the age of the test purchase volunteer.[7]

Where a person is charged with an offence by reason of his own conduct under this section, it is a defence for him to demonstrate that he believed the individual to be over 18 and either had asked the individual his age and the evidence provided would have convinced a reasonable person or nobody could reasonably have suspected from the individual's appearance that he was aged under 18. In the case of test purchase volunteers, the individual's appearance is best judged by a photograph taken at the time (usually on the same day) as the offence. Unless proceedings are started quickly and expedited through the courts, any comparison of the test purchase volunteer's appearance at the date of trial and their appearance on the date of the offence would be impracticable. Photographs taken on the day provide the best evidence[8].

Where a person is charged with an offence by reason of the act or default of another, it is a defence for him to demonstrate that he exercised all due diligence to avoid committing it. For more information on reasonable precautions and due diligence, see chapter ten, *post*.

By section 147 a person commits an offence if he knowingly allows the sale of alcohol on licensed premises to an individual aged under 18 years. The offence only applies to a person working at the premises in a capacity, paid or unpaid, which authorises him to prevent the sale. A similar offence applies to club members in a club premises.

A reasonable and bona fide belief that the individual is over 18 will be a valid defence under S.147. It is for the prosecutor to prove that the offender knew the individual was under 18[9]. Knowledge cannot be imputed from a poor system or that it was inevitable that persons under 18 would gain entry and buy alcohol

---

[6] Family Law Reform Act 1969, S.9(1). The time at which a person attains a particular age expressed in years shall be the commencement of the relevant anniversary of the date of his birth.

[7] However, see now new guidance on evidence of birth date on page 162, *post*

[8] *R (Verma) v Stratford Magistrates' Court* [2006] EWHC 715 (Admin)

[9] *Sherras v De Rutzen* [1895] 1 QB 918

due to the systems operated[10]. However, knowledge can be imputed by the seller 'turning a blind eye' to the obvious[11]. A licensee can still be liable for the actions of his manager or servants even where they have sold or supplied liquor contrary to the licensee's express general instructions[12].

There is no automatic liability under S.146 or S.147 for the designated premises supervisor (as opposed to the premises licence holder) unless they make the sale (under S.146(1)) or have the requisite knowledge of a sale (under S.147(1))[13].

By section 147A[14], the holder of a premises licence (or premises user for a temporary event notice) will commit an offence if on two or more occasions within three consecutive months alcohol is unlawfully sold to an individual under 18 years. It can be different sellers and buyers on each occasion, but it must be on the same premises. The same sale may not be counted towards more than one offence and may not be used for charging offences under both S.146 or S.147 and S.147A.

In determining whether alcohol is sold on two or more occasions within three consecutive months, the court may admit evidence that a person has been convicted of an offence under S.146 (but not S.147) relating to that premises; that a person has accepted a formal caution[15] in respect of such an offence; or that a person has paid a fixed penalty notice in relation to such an offence (see section 2.12, *post* for more about fixed penalties). In addition, if convicted of an offence of persistently selling alcohol to children, a court can suspend a licence for up to three months without the need for a formal review before the Licensing Authority (see section 2.7, *post* for more about licence reviews).

By section 151 a person who works on licensed premises in any capacity, whether paid or unpaid, commits an offence if he knowingly delivers alcohol sold on the premises (or supplied by a club) to a person aged under 18 years.

Similarly, an offence is committed by a person who works on licensed premises in any capacity, whether paid or unpaid, if they knowingly allow someone else to so deliver alcohol. This offence can be linked to proxy sales (see section 2.9 *post*), so where, for instance, a member of bar staff knows that a purchaser of alcohol who is over 18 is going to deliver it to someone who is under 18, it would be an offence.

---

[10] *Buxton v Chief Constable of Northumbria* (1983) 148 JP 9
[11] *R v Cohen* [1951] 1 All ER 203
[12] *Commissioner of Police v Cartman* [1896] 1 QB 655
[13] Hertfordshire CC v Bastwick [2007] WLR 729
[14] Added by S.23 Violent Crime Reduction Act 2006.
[15] In order to be a 'formal caution' it must be issued in accordance with Part 5 of the Police Act 1997

2.6      Age Verification Policies

In October 2010, the government introduced a mandatory condition[16] applied to all alcohol licences requiring an age verification policy to be in place. On 1st October 2014[17], this was updated to include provisions making the designated premises supervisor personally responsible for ensuring supply of alcohol is carried on in accordance with the age verification policy. This potentially means that, whilst a designated premises supervisor is not directly liable for an under age sale of alcohol (unless they were the actual seller or knew about the sale), they could be liable for failing to implement an age verification policy.

The mandatory condition states:

(1)      The premises licence holder or club premises certificate holder must ensure that an age verification policy is adopted in respect of the premises in relation to the sale or supply of alcohol.

(2)      The designated premises supervisor in relation to the premises licence must ensure that the supply of alcohol at the premises is carried on in accordance with the age verification policy.

(3)      The policy must require individuals who appear to the responsible person to be under 18 years of age (or such older age as may be specified in the policy) to produce on request, before being served alcohol, identification bearing their photograph, date of birth and either—

(a)      a holographic mark, or
(b)      an ultraviolet feature

The condition applies to companies that sell alcohol remotely (for example, online or by mail order). Since the condition requires that identification is produced on request, before alcohol is served, photo ID should be shown at or before the point of service.

The failure to have an Age Verification Policy in place is not a direct offence, but would be a breach of a licence condition under s.136(1) of the Licensing Act 2003.

---

[16] S.19(2), Licensing Act 2003 and Licensing Act (Mandatory Licensing Conditions) Order 2010: SI2010:860
[17] Schedule 1, Paragraph 3 Licensing Act 2003 (Mandatory Licensing Conditions) (Amendment) Order 2014

2.7      Licensing Review

A responsible body under the Licensing Act 2003, which includes amongst others, the local police, Trading Standards Department and Licensing Authority, can commence a review of a licence if they can demonstrate that one of the licensing objectives has been breached. The relevant objective here is the 'protection of children from harm'. The process of licence review is outside the scope of this book, but is often used by local Trading Standards either instead of or in addition to prosecution for offences.

Licensing Authorities have the power to revoke, suspend or amend licences, can add conditions to licences or can issue warnings. Often conditions can be framed around the acceptable best practice and, it should be noted that, if attached as conditions, the best practice will become mandatory rather that discretionary.

When reviewing a licence to sell alcohol on the grounds of criminal activity including the sale of alcohol to minors, it is appropriate and necessary to consider the wider public interest and the furtherance of the licensing objectives, which included the prevention of crime[18].

2.8      Liqueur Confectionary

From 26th May 2015, s.70 of the Deregulation Act 2015 abolished the offence of selling liqueur confectionary to a person aged under 16.

Liqueur confectionary is confectionary that contains less than 200ml of alcohol (less than 57% by volume in strength) per kg of chocolate and each piece of confectionary is not more than 42g in weight, or is designed to be broken into such sized pieces prior to consumption[19]. Any products with concentrations above this level would be considered to be alcohol and therefore covered by the general prohibition on sales to under 18's.

2.9      Proxy Sales

A person commits an offence if he buys or attempts to buy alcohol for a person aged under 18 years. This is commonly referred to as 'proxy sales'. There is a similar offence for supplies taking place on club premises.

---

[18] R (on the application of Bassetlaw DC) v Worksop Magistrates' Court [2008] EWHC 3530 (Admin)
[19] S.191(1), Licensing Act 2003

It is a defence for the person charged to demonstrate that they had no reason to suspect that the person was aged under 18 years.

In licensed premises, a person aged over 18 is exempt from the offence of buying alcohol on behalf of a person aged 16 or 17, if:

- The alcohol is beer, wine or cider (but not spirits)
- It is for consumption on the premises with a table meal[20], and
- The person is accompanied by a person aged 18 years or more

Similarly, the individual aged 16 or 17 is exempt from the offence of consuming alcohol in licensed premises under those circumstances.

Those aged 16 to 18 can consume alcohol with a meal and can do so in an area set aside for food or in a bar area. The law specifies that people between the ages of 16 and 18 can drink wine, beer or cider with a table meal as long as the drink is purchased by an adult. This can take place anywhere in the premises, including the bar or an area set aside as a restaurant. This is different from the law under the Licensing Act 1964. It should be noted, however, that 16 year olds cannot purchase their own alcoholic drink when consuming a meal. There still remains the strict liability offence of adults buying alcohol on behalf of young people, i.e. taking money from them, buying the alcohol and then giving the alcohol back to them. Adults are quite properly allowed to buy drinks for those aged between 16 and 18 with a meal, but not as an agent.

2.10    Attempted Purchase, Possession and Consumption by Children

By section 149 (1) of the Licensing Act 2003, an individual aged under 18 commits an offence if he buys or attempts to buy alcohol. There is a similar offence for supplies taking place on club premises.

In order to be tried for this offence, the individual must be at least 10 years of age[21].

This offence does not apply to test purchase volunteers instructed by a Trading Standards Officer (who for the purposes of this Act must be a Weights and Measures Inspector[22]) or a Police Officer.

---

[20] A substantial sandwich accompanied by beetroot and pickles was held to be a 'table meal' in *Timmis v Millman* [1965] Crim LR 107

[21] S.50, Children and Young Persons Act 1933

[22] Not all 'Trading Standards Officers' are formally qualified under S.73 of the Weights and Measures Act 1985

By section 150 (1) an individual aged under 18 commits an offence if he consumes alcohol in a licensed premises or club premises. This offence does not apply to individuals aged 16 or 17 in circumstances as set out in section 2.9 *ante*.

By section 152 (1) a person commits an offence if they knowingly send an individual aged under 18 to obtain alcohol for consumption off the premises (or off a club premises). This offence does not apply to test purchase volunteers instructed by Trading Standards or the police.

By section 5(1) of the Children and Young Persons Act 1933, a person commits an offence if they give alcohol to a child under the age of 5 years. This is except upon the order of a duly qualified medical practitioner, or in case of sickness, apprehended sickness, or other urgent cause. The penalty is a fine of up to £200.

## 2.11   Enforcement

The enforcement of these provisions is split between Trading Standards and the police. In general, Trading Standards Officers enforce the provisions of section 146 (Sale of Alcohol to Children), section 147 (Knowingly Allowing the Sale of Alcohol to Children) and section 147A (Persistently Selling Alcohol to Children)[23].

All of the other offences are generally enforced by the police, but local variations do apply.

Proceedings may be instituted up to 12 months after the commission of the offence[24], except for the offence of giving alcohol to a child under 5, which may be instituted up to 6 months after the commission of the offence.

## 2.12   Penalties

The penalties for offences are expressed as maximum levels based upon the standard scale[25] applicable in Magistrates' Courts. All of the offences set out in this section are 'summary only' and may only be tried in the Magistrates' Courts.

---

[23] S.182(2)(c), Licensing Act 2003
[24] S.186(3), Licensing Act 2003
[25] S.37(2), Criminal Justice Act 1982 as amended by s.85 of the Legal Aid, Sentencing and Punishment of Offenders Act 2012

CYPA1933 – Children and Young Persons Act 1933
LA2003 – Licensing Act 2003

Level One - £200 maximum

S.5(1) – CYPA1933 – Giving Alcohol to a Child under 5 years

Level Two - £500 maximum

Level Three - £1,000 maximum

S.145(1) – LA2003 – Allowing an unaccompanied child on licensed premises
S.149(1) – LA2003 – A person aged under 18 buying or attempting to buy alcohol
S.150(1) – LA2003 – A person aged under 18 knowingly consuming alcohol on licensed premises

Level Four - £2,500 maximum

Level Five – unlimited fine

S.146(1) – LA2003 – Sale of Alcohol to an Individual under 18 in licensed premises
S.146(2) – LA2003 – Supply of Alcohol to an Individual under 18 by a club
S.146(3) – LA2003 – Supply of Alcohol to an Individual under 18 on behalf of a club
S.147(1) – LA2003 – Knowingly allowing the Supply of Alcohol to an Individual under 18 in licensed premises
S.147(3) – LA2003 – Knowingly allowing the Supply of Alcohol to an individual under 18 by or on behalf of a club
S.149(3) – LA2003 – Buying or Attempting to Buy Alcohol on Behalf of a Person under 18 years
S.149(4) – LA2003 – Supplying Alcohol to a Person under 18 years
S.150(2) – LA2003 – Knowingly allowing the consumption of alcohol by a person under 18 years on licensed premises
S.151(1) – LA2003 – Workers knowingly delivering alcohol to a person under 18 years
S.151(2) – LA2003 – Workers knowingly allowing somebody else to deliver alcohol to a person under 18 years in licensed premises
S.151(4) – LA2003 – Workers knowingly allowing somebody else to deliver alcohol to a person under 18 years in a club premises
S.152(1) – LA2003 – Knowingly sending an individual aged under 18 to obtain alcohol

General - unlimited fine

S.147(1) – LA2003 – Persistently selling Alcohol to Children[26]
S.136(1) – LA2003 – Operating otherwise than in accordance with an authorisation (licence) – such as failing to have a mandatory age verification policy in place (Note: this offence also carries a potential prison sentence of up to 6 months in addition to or instead of a fine)

Penalty Notice for Disorder

A penalty notice for disorder (PND) is a type of fixed penalty notice that can be issued for the offence of supplying alcohol to a person under the age of 18 years.
The PND scheme was introduced under the Criminal Justice and Police Act 2001 as part of the government's strategy to provide police with a swift financial punishment to deal with misbehaviour and a practical deterrent to future re-offending.

The Home Office says that the aims of the scheme are to:

- Offer operational officers a new, effective alternative means of dealing with low-level, anti-social and nuisance offending
- Deliver swift, simple and effective justice that carries a deterrent effect
- Reduce the amount of time that police officers spend on completing paperwork and attending court, while simultaneously reducing the burden on the courts
- Increase the amount of time officers spend on the street dealing with more serious crime and to free the courts to deal with more serious offending

A PND may be issued by a police constable, a police community support officer or an 'accredited person'. The Police and Justice Act 2006 specifically extended the range of those who may be directly accredited to Trading Standards Officers (TSOs) for the purpose of issuing penalty notices for selling alcohol to a person under the age of 18. However, not all areas have been accredited by the local chief officer of police to issue such notices, so local practices vary.

The PND penalty is currently fixed at £90.

---

[20] The penalty for this offence was increased from 12th March 2015,  from £10,000 to £20,000 with effect from 25th April 2012 by the Police Reform and Social Responsibility Act 2010 and made unlimited by s.85 of the Legal Aid, Sentencing and Punishment of Offenders Act 2012.

CHAPTER THREE

# TOBACCO

## CONTENTS

## 3.1    Introduction

Tobacco controls are changing rapidly as the government introduce tighter regulations as a part of their tobacco control strategy. The rules on under age sales of tobacco are found in the Children and Young Persons Act 1933, Children and Young Persons (Protection from Tobacco) Act 1991 and the Children and Young Persons (Sale of Tobacco) Order 2007.

In 2004, the government published a white paper called *Choosing Health*. This set out a roadmap for strengthening controls on tobacco marketing, advertising, promotion and sale. This book is only concerned with the age restricted sales aspects of that, but the government have also introduced bans on vending machines, pictorial warnings on cigarette packaging, bans on smoking in public places and many other measures aimed at reducing smoking. Many local areas and regions have also introduced smoke free task forces and tobacco control strategies. Smoke Free North West, for example, aims to 'Make smoking history for our children'.

## 3.2    Key Legislation

Children and Young Persons Act 1933
Children and Young Persons (Protection from Tobacco) Act 1991
Tobacco Advertising and Promotions Act 2002
Children and Families Act 2014

## 3.3    Summary of Age Restricted Laws relating to Tobacco

- Tobacco products must not be sold to a person under the age of 18 years
- Vendors of tobacco products must display a sign of at least A3 in size stating 'It is illegal to sell tobacco to anyone under the age of 18'
- It is a defence for the person charged to prove that they took all reasonable precautions and exercised all due diligence to avoid commission of the offence
- The sales offence carries a penalty of £2,500; failure to display the statutory notice carries a penalty of £1,000
- Cigarette lighter refill canisters must not be sold to a person under the age of 18 years (see section 6.6, post)
- Matches, whilst commonly sold with tobacco products, are not age restricted.

- Tobacco products may not be displayed to any person under the age of 18
- A tobacco product price list may not be displayed to any person under the age of 18
- Nicotine Inhaling Products (such as e-cigarettes) may not be sold to any person under the age of 18 unless they are a specified medicine or medical device authorised for use by under 18's.

3.4     Tobacco Products

Tobacco means[1] any product containing tobacco including cigarettes, tobacco for oral or nasal use and smoking mixtures intended as an alternative to tobacco. Cigarettes include cut tobacco rolled up in paper, tobacco leaf or other material in such form as to be capable for use for immediate smoking.

The definition includes smokeless tobacco, which is common in countries like Bangladesh, Egypt, Turkey, India and Pakistan – together with other Middle Eastern countries. This tobacco is imported into the UK and is covered by the age restrictions.

The age restrictions also apply to cigarette papers.

3.5     Matches and Lighters

Matches, matchbooks and lighters are not age restricted products.

However, many retailers place voluntary restrictions on items like matches, fire-lighters, lighting gel and similar fire starting products. This is perfectly lawful (see section 9.15, *post*).

It should be noted that whilst lighters themselves are not age restricted, the cigarette lighter refill canisters are (see section 6.6, *post*).

3.6     Sale of Tobacco Products to Children

Section 7 of the Children and Young Persons Act 1933 prohibits the sale of tobacco or cigarette papers to any person under the age of 18 years.

The restrictions do not apply to the supply of tobacco or cigarette papers to any person who is employed by a tobacco manufacturer or tobacco dealer. This

---

[1] S.7(5), Children and Young Persons Act 1933

would indicate that a member of staff purchasing tobacco from their employer (even if they are under 18) would not generate an offence. However, the purchase has to be for the purpose of their business and consequently not for personal consumption.

In addition, a messenger boy employed by a messenger company (provided he is in uniform) is exempt from the legislation.

This is an offence of strict liability; it is immaterial whether or not the shopkeeper knew that the sale was taking place[2]. It is a defence for the person charged to prove that he took all reasonable precautions and exercised all due diligence to avoid the commission of the offence (see chapter ten, *post*)[3].

3.7     Mandatory Warning Notices

By section 4(1) of the Children and Young Persons (Protection from Tobacco) Act 1991, it is an offence for any person to carry on a business involving the retail of tobacco and to fail to display a mandatory warning notice.

The notice must be displayed in a prominent position where it is readily visible to persons at the point of sale. The notice must state:

> *'It is illegal to sell tobacco products to anyone under the age of 18'*

No alternate forms of words are permitted. By the Protection from Tobacco (Display of Warning Statements) Regulations 1992, the notice must not be less than 297mm by 420mm (A3 size paper) and the characters shall not be less than 36mm high.

The notice must be displayed wherever tobacco is retailed and includes, for instance, ice cream vans, mobile traders, market stalls, any vehicle, vessel, aircraft, hovercraft, stall or moveable structure.

It is a defence for the person charged to prove that he took all reasonable precautions and exercised all due diligence to avoid the commission of the offence (see chapter ten, *post*).

---

[2] St. Helens MBC v Hill (1992) 156 JP 602

[3] A decision to acquit a defendant on the basis of having taken 'all reasonable precautions' when there were other things the defendant could have done, is not necessarily perverse – see more in chapter ten, *post* – *Hereford & Worcester County Council v T & S Stores plc* (1994) 93 LGR 98

If the offence is committed by a body corporate and is proved to have been committed with the consent or connivance of, or attributable to the neglect on the part of, any director, manager, secretary, or other similar officer of the body corporate, or any other person purporting to act in such a capacity, he as well as the body corporate shall be guilty of that offence. Many small retail shops are set up through limited companies, so these provisions can be important to attach criminal liability to the directors of the company for their fault. However, the apparently broad scope of this provision is limited by case law to only those who are in a position of real authority. It is to catch those responsible for putting the company procedures in place[4].

3.8    Tobacco Display Ban

It is an offence for a retailer to openly display tobacco to the public in any store, except for specialist tobacconists provided tobacco cannot be viewed from outside the store[5]. This book does not cover the specifics of the display ban except for those aspects relating to displaying tobacco to children.

By s.7A (2) of the Tobacco Advertising and Promotions Act 2002 a tobacco display is permitted if the display is a requested display to an individual aged 18 or over. If a person unlawfully displays tobacco to an individual aged under 18 it is a defence that they believed that the individual was aged 18 or over, and they had taken reasonable steps to establish the individual's age or from the individual's appearance nobody could reasonably have suspected that the individual was aged under 18. A person is treated as having taken all reasonable steps to establish an individual's age if the person asked the individual for evidence of the individual's age, and the evidence would have convinced a reasonable person.

Where a person causes the display of the tobacco product it is a defence that they exercised all due diligence to avoid committing the offence.

The Association of Convenience Stores together with their Primary Authority, Surrey County Council, have produced some assured advice under the terms of the Regulatory Enforcement and Sanctions Act 2008. In that advice, it is permissible to open the covered display in response to a request from an adult even if they are accompanied by a child. It is also permissible to open the display for restocking, maintenance, cleaning and training[6].

---

[4] *R v Boal* [1992] 1 QB 591
[5] S.7A Tobacco Advertising and Promotion Act 2002 as inserted by s.21 Health Act 2009
[6] See Tobacco Advertising and Promotion (Display) (England) Regulations 2010 (SI 2010:445)

The Tobacco Advertising and Promotion (Display of Prices) (England) Regulations 2010[7] prohibit the display of a counter tobacco catalogue to any person under the age of 18. However, a limited size display unit poster and/or shelf edge price labels are permitted to be displayed. By Regulation 7(1) the counter tobacco catalogue may display prices of tobacco products in the form of a price list which is made available to an individual aged 18 or over following a particular request by the individual for information about tobacco products for sale in the place where such request takes place.

The seller must take all reasonable steps to ensure that the individual making such a request is aged 18 or over before such a display takes place and the display lasts for no longer than is needed for the individual to obtain the information sought by the buyer.

There are strict rules concerning the layout of the price list including font sizes and types, pictorial displays and promotional wording. Only one price list is permitted per till.

There is a similar due diligence defence available to that outlined in S.7A (2) above.

3.9     Nicotine Inhaling Products (E-cigarettes)

The Nicotine Inhaling Products (Age of Sale and Proxy Purchasing) Regulations 2015 made under s.92 of the Children and Families Act 2014 prohibit the sale of a nicotine inhaling product, commonly referred to as an e-cigarette or electronic cigarette, to any person under the age of 18.

A nicotine inhaling product includes:

- a nicotine cartridge which contains a substance which is not tobacco but consists of, or contains, nicotine, and is intended to form part of a nicotine inhaling device
- a nicotine inhaling device which is intended to enable nicotine to be inhaled through a mouth piece (regardless of whether the device is also intended to enable any other substance to be inhaled through a mouth piece), but is not tobacco, cigarette papers or a device intended to be used for the consumption of lit tobacco
- a nicotine refill substance which is not tobacco but consists of, or contains, nicotine, and is intended to be used to refill a nicotine inhaling device

---

[7] SI 2010:863

A "nicotine product" is

- a device which is intended to enable nicotine to be consumed by an individual or otherwise to be delivered into the human body
- an item which is intended to form part of such a device, or
- a substance or item which consists of or contains nicotine and which is intended for human consumption or otherwise to be delivered into the human body.

It does not matter whether the device is also intended to enable any other substance to be consumed by an individual or otherwise to be delivered into the human body.

Some medicinal products are exempt, in certain circumstances from the prohibition.

Where a nicotine inhaling product is a medicinal product or medical device[8] available under prescription in accordance with Part 12 of the Human Medicines Regulations 2012[9], it is exempt from the prohibition on the basis that the doctor prescribing the product and the pharmacist dispensing it is acting in the medical interests of the child – such as when they are attempting to quit smoking.

A further confusion arises from the possibility that a marketing authorisation[10] may exist from the Medicines and Healthcare Regulatory Agency or a parallel import licence[11] may exist. In such circumstances the authorised medicinal product may have an indication in its summary of product characteristics that it is indicated for the treatment of persons under 18. These products can be on general sale in non-pharmacy premises and do not require a prescription.

The prohibition on supply to under 18's will not apply to these authorised medicinal products provided the age of the person to whom the product was supplied was within the parameters of the summary of product characteristics indication. This would mean, for instance, that if the product indicated that it was suitable for over 16's, then the prohibition in the Nicotine Inhaling Devices Regulations would not apply provided the buyer was aged 16 or 17. However, if the buyer was under 16 then the exemption would not apply and the

---

[8] Medical Devices Regulations 2002 (SI2002:618)
[9] (SI2012:1916) as amended
[10] R. 8(1) Human Medicines Regulations 2012
[11] R. 48(2) Human Medicines Regulations 2012

prohibition would stand. This could prove to be rather confusing for retailers, but the government were clear that they did not want to impede young people accessing authorised medical products that may assist them to stop smoking tobacco.

The prohibition does not apply to transactions between nicotine inhaling product manufacturers and dealers and persons in the trade.

There is a statutory defence available of taking all reasonable precautions and exercised all due diligence to avoid committing the offence.

The penalty for breaching the prohibition is a fine up to £2,500.

3.10    Restricted Premises Orders and Restricted Sale Orders

On 1st April 2009, new sanctions for the persistent illegal sales of tobacco were introduced[12]. The sanctions may be imposed after relevant convictions by local magistrates, but only if requested by the prosecutor. It is a form of negative licensing (i.e. banning a location or person from retailing tobacco).

The sanctions may be sought only where there have been persistent illegal sales of tobacco or nicotine inhaling products made to young people. They apply where a person is convicted of making an illegal sale to a young person under the age of 18 years and there have been at least two other occasions within the preceding two years that the person has committed similar offences in relation to the particular premises.

A restricted premises order means that the retail business at the location where the offence took place is prohibited from selling tobacco or nicotine inhaling products for a period of up to one year. This applies to a specific premise, so would not apply to any other stores in a company or retail chain.

A restricted sale order means that a named person within a business is prohibited from selling tobacco or from having any management role in any premises relating to tobacco sales within a business for a period of up to one year. This order attaches to the individual regardless of where they are employed.

---

[12] S.143, Criminal Justice and Immigration Act 2008

The applicant, usually a local Trading Standards Department, for any of these orders must give written notice of the application to every person appearing to them to be affected by it. This is likely to include the owner of the premises and the employees at the premises. There may also be commercial arrangements in place tying provision of certain services (such as provision of display gantries) to levels of tobacco or nicotine inhaling product sales and the parties to those agreements would also need to be served with notice of the application. No timescale for the notice is provided in the legislation, but would be expected to be a reasonable time to enable a person affected by the order to make representations to the court. A person not given notice of the application, but affected by it, can apply to the court subsequently for an order varying or discharging the original order. An appeal against the order, refusal to vary or discharge it or refusal to grant it lies to the Crown Court.

The application can only be made following a conviction for a tobacco or nicotine inhaling product offence (see section 3.6 + 3.9, *ante*), but the antecedents relied upon to justify the order do not have to be convictions. The applicant merely has to show that the two prior offences were 'committed'. This could be shown, for instance, by the acceptance of a formal caution[13], the acceptance and payment of a penalty notice[14] or (unlike the offence of persistently selling alcohol) by the issuing of a warning letter following an illegal sale. However, if no further action was taken following an illegal sale, this will not count towards the number.

A restricted premises order is a local land charge, so is recorded on the land registry. If the business is sold during the timespan for the order, it will continue to apply to the new owner unless they apply to the magistrates for an order to discharge it.

By section 12C(1) of the Children and Young Persons Act 1933, if a person sells on any premises any tobacco, cigarette papers or nicotine inhaling product in contravention of a restricted premises order and they knew, or ought reasonably to have known that the sale was a contravention of the order, they commit an offence.

By section 12C(2), if a person fails to comply with a restricted sale order, they commit an offence. However, it is a defence for them to prove that they took all reasonable precautions and exercised all due diligence to avoid the commission of the offence (See chapter ten, *post*).

---

[13] In order to be a 'formal caution' it must be issued in accordance with Part 5 of the Police Act 1997
[14] See section 3.12, *post*

3.11    Proxy Sales

By s.91 of the Children and Families Act 2014 a person commits an offence if he buys or attempts to buy tobacco, cigarette papers or a relevant nicotine product for a person aged under 18 years. This is commonly referred to as 'proxy sales'.

It is a defence for the person charged to demonstrate that they had no reason to suspect that the person was aged under 18 years.

It is also a defence in a case where the person has bought or attempted to buy cigarette papers, that the person had no reason to suspect that the individual concerned intended to use the papers for smoking.

The penalty for a proxy sales offence is a fine up to £2,500.

3.12    Enforcement

There is no duty on local authorities to enforce the restrictions on tobacco products, but by section 5 of the Children and Young Persons (Protection from Tobacco) Act 1991, local authorities are required to consider every year the extent to which it is appropriate to carry out a programme of enforcement action in their area and to carry out such a programme.

Trading Standards Officers are not granted any specific powers of entry or investigation in connection with tobacco offences.

However, s.91(4) of the Children and Families Act 2014 says that a local weights and measures authority (Trading Standards)  must enforce the provisions relating to proxy purchasing. The Act gives officers powers to issue fixed penalty notices. This is an unusual provision as Trading Standards Officers are not usually engaged in enforcement activity against members of the public, as opposed to against those engaged in a trade or business.

These provisions will present some challenges for TSO's as, although the Act provides for the issue of a fixed penalty notice by the officer, they have no powers to stop a member of public in the street to ascertain their identity. It would seem that these offences will require the assistance of a police officer to be practically enforceable.

3.13   Penalties

The penalties for offences are expressed as maximum levels based upon the standard scale[15] applicable in Magistrates' Courts. All of the offences set out in this section are 'summary only' and may only be tried in the Magistrates' Courts.

CYPA1933 - Children and Young Persons Act 1933
TAPA2002 - Tobacco Advertising and Promotion Act 2002
CFA2014 - Children and Families Act 2014

Level One - £200 maximum

Level Two - £500 maximum

Level Three - £1,000 maximum

S.4(1) CYPA1933 – Failure to Display a Statutory Tobacco Notice

Level Four - £2,500 maximum

S.7(1) CYPA1933 – Sale of Tobacco Products to a person aged under 18

S.92 - CFA2014 - Sale of nicotine inhaling product to a person aged under 18
S.91 - CFA2014 - Buying or attempting to buy tobacco or a nicotine product for a person aged under 18.

Level Five - unlimited fine

S.7A(2) - TAPA2002 - Displaying tobacco to a person under 18
S.7C(2) - TAPA2002 - Displaying a tobacco counter price list to a person under 18

General - unlimited fine

S.12C(1) CYPA1933 – Failure to comply with a Restricted Premises Order
S.12C(2) CYPA1933 – Failure to comply with a Restricted Sales Order

---

[15] S.37(2), Criminal Justice Act 1982  as amended by s.85 of the Legal Aid, Sentencing and Punishment of Offenders Act 2012

CHAPTER FOUR

# KNIVES, OFFENSIVE WEAPONS AND FIREARMS

**CONTENTS**

4.1       Introduction

The UK has some of the most restrictive laws on the sale and supply of weapons anywhere in the world. These are particularly restrictive when concerning children and young people.

4.2       Key Legislation

Crossbows Act 1987
Criminal Justice Act 1988
Firearms Act 1968

4.3       Summary of Age Restricted Laws relating to Knives, Offensive Weapons and Firearms

- Knives and bladed instruments must not be sold to a person under the age of 18 years
- Certain types of knives are illegal to sell to anyone
- Some bladed instruments or sharp pointed instruments like skewers, scissors, safety razors and wooden or plastic cutlery are exempt
- It is a defence for the person charged to prove that they took all reasonable precautions and exercised all due diligence to avoid commission of the offence
- There are also defences available for certain antiques and curios
- The above offences carry an unlimited fine and/or up to six months in prison
- Crossbows must not be sold to a person under the age of 18 years
- Parts for crossbows, including arrows, may not be sold or let for hire to a person under the age of 18 years
- A person under the age of 18 years may not purchase or hire a crossbow
- A person under the age of 18 years may not possess a crossbow or parts for a crossbow unless they are accompanied by a person over the age of 21 years
- There are exemptions for 'low power' crossbows (often found in toys)
- It is a defence for a person who sold or let for hire a crossbow to demonstrate that they reasonably believed the buyer or hirer to be over 18 years of age

- The penalty for a breach by a seller is an unlimited fine and/or imprisonment for up to six months. The maximum penalty for a buyer or hirer is a maximum £1,000 fine
- A court may order the forfeiture of the crossbow, but has no powers to prevent a shop from continuing to sell crossbows in the future
- Firearms (including air rifles) and ammunition must not be sold or hired to a person under the age of 18 years
- A person under the age of 14 years may not possess a firearm or ammunition, but a person aged 14 – 18 years may possess them on private property with permission and under the supervision of a person aged over 21 years
- A realistic imitation firearm, if sold under one of the exemptions from prohibition, must not be sold or hired to a person under the age of 18 years
- An imitation firearm made unrealistic may not be sold or hired to a person under the age of 18 years
- Some 'firearm-shaped' objects are so obviously not firearms that they are not restricted, examples include 'super soaker water pistols' or 'futuristic space weapons'

## 4.4   Knives

It is important to establish what legal category of knife the product falls into. This is because it may be illegal to sell it at all, illegal to sell it to anyone under the age of 18 years or legal to sell it to anyone.

There is such a broad range of products that fall within the definition of knives, that it is perhaps easier to describe items that fall outside the legislation.

The following items are not considered to be knives for the purposes of this legislation:

- A folding pocket knife, if the cutting edge of the blade is less than 3 inches or 7.62cm
- A replacement cartridge for safety razors where less than 2mm of the blade is exposed
- Skewers
- Screw drivers[1]
- Scissors
- Certain types of saws with blunt points (like pruning saws or plasterboard saws)

---

[1] R v Davis [1998] Crim LR 564

- Fruit peelers (however a 'grapefruit knife' has been held to be a knife for this legislation[2])
- Children's cutlery
- Wooden or plastic cutlery

There are certain types of knives that it is illegal to sell to any person (with some narrow exceptions[3]). It is also illegal to import these knives, so the result is that they are practically unavailable to buy in the UK. However, they can still be found on the internet and retailers in the UK need to be aware of the restrictions on their importation. The following are knives that cannot be sold to anyone unless the knife is more than 100 years old at the time of sale[4]:

- A 'swordstick', that is, a hollow walking-stick or cane containing a blade which may be used as a sword
- A 'handclaw', being a band of metal or other hard material from which a number of sharp spikes protrude, worn around the hand
- A 'belt buckle knife', being a buckle which incorporates or conceals a knife
- A 'push dagger', being a knife the handle of which fits within a clenched fist and the blade of which protrudes from between two fingers
- A 'hollow kubotan', being a cylindrical container containing a number of sharp spikes
- A 'footclaw', being a bar of metal or other hard material from which a number of sharp spikes protrude, worn strapped to the foot
- A 'shuriken', 'shaken' or 'death star', being a hard, non-flexible plate having three or more sharp radiating points and designed to be thrown
- A 'balisong' or 'butterfly knife', being a blade enclosed by its handle, which is designed to split down the middle without the operation of a spring or other mechanical means, to reveal the blade
- A 'kusari gama', being a length of rope, cord, wire or chain fastened at one end to a sickle
- A 'kyoketsu shoge', being a length of rope, cord, wire or chain fastened at one end to a hooked knife
- A 'manrikigusari' or 'kusari', being a length of rope, cord, wire or chain fastened at each end to a hard weight or hand grip

In addition, by virtue of the Restriction of Offensive Weapons Act 1959:

- A 'flick knife' or 'flick gun', being a blade which opens automatically by hand

---

[2] *R (Windsor & Maidenhead Borough Council) v East Berkshire Magistrates' Court* [2010] EWHC 3020 (Admin)
[3] See S.141 (5), (8) and (11A) of the Criminal Justice Act 1988 (c.33)
[4] Criminal Justice Act 1988 (Offensive Weapons) Order 1988

pressure applied to a button, spring or other device in or attached to the handle of the knife

- A 'gravity knife', being a blade which is released from the handle or sheath thereof by the force of gravity of the application of centrifugal force and which, when released, is locked in place by means of a button, spring lever, or other device

Everything else, falling between those categories, is a knife and, by S.141A(1) of the Criminal Justice Act 1988 is illegal to sell to any person under the age of 18 years.

A small folding pocket knife, where the cutting edge of the blade is less than 3 inches or 7.62cm is exempt from the legislation, by virtue of the Criminal Justice Act 1988 (Offensive Weapons) (Exemption) Order 1996[5].

Sellers should exercise care with this definition, as it is important that the blade must be 'non-locking'. This means that it must be readily and immediately foldable at all times, simply by the folding process. A lock-knife, which required a further process, namely activating a trigger mechanism to fold the blade back into the handle, was held not to be a folding pocket knife[6], a decision approved by the Court of Appeal[7].

Many 'Swiss Army Knives' have locking mechanisms on their blades and these are both illegal to sell to children and illegal to possess in a public place without good reason or lawful authority. In one case, a retired chief inspector was prosecuted when found with a locking Swiss Army Knife in his luggage at East Midlands Airport. He was eventually cleared, but the case shows that the Crown Prosecution Service adopt a narrow interpretation of locking knives.

A safety razor blade is exempt from the legislation by virtue of the Criminal Justice Act 1988 (Offensive Weapons) (Exemption) Order 1996. To be exempt the blade must be permanently enclosed in a cartridge or housing and the blades must not protrude more than 2mm from the highest point of the cartridge or housing. It is important to note that not all safety razors comply with this definition.

There is no offence for purchasing a knife for use by a person under the age of

---

[5] SI 1996/3064
[6] *Harris v DPP* [1993] 1 All ER 562
[7] *R v Deegan* [1998] Crim LR 562; [1998] 2 Cr App Rep 121

18 years. This is commonly known as proxy sales. This has proved problematic for parents of children embarking on cookery or catering courses at college. It is illegal to directly sell those knives to those children, so often their parents or guardians attend at the shop and purchase the catering knives on behalf of their children. This is lawful.

The seller of a knife has no authority to ask what reason the knife is for, or who it is for, and the purchaser is under no obligation to inform the seller of the knives intended use. However, a seller is within their rights to refuse to sell the knife at all if, for whatever reason, they are unhappy with the sale on personal, moral or community safety grounds. This right derives from the law of contract, in that, when a buyer says they would like to buy a knife, they make an 'offer' to buy the knife and enter into a contract with the seller. However, the seller is not under any obligation to accept the offer and, until they do, no contract is formed. In other words, the seller can simply refuse to enter into a contract with the buyer.

It should be noted that, if challenged, the purchaser of a knife carried in a public place must provide a police officer with good reason or lawful authority for having the knife with them in a public place[8]. This is regardless of whether or not it remains in its packaging as supplied by the seller.

By section 141A(4), it is a defence for the person charged to prove that he took all reasonable precautions and exercised all due diligence to avoid the commission of the offence. The scope of acceptable precautions was explored in some detail by the High Court in *London Borough of Croydon v Pinch-a-Pound* [9], a case discussed in more detail in chapter ten, *post*.

4.5     Crossbows

A crossbow is a form of bow in which the bow-stave (prod) is fixed crosswise to a stock. The bow can then be spanned back by hand or by means of a lever or windlass, and the string held in place by a catch that is released by a trigger to shoot an arrow, bolt or quarrel. The crossbow must have a minimum draw weight of 1.4kg, less powerful crossbows are not restricted (which would include 'toys' with the appearance of being a crossbow). Crossbows are not firearms for legislative purposes unless they are constructed to incorporate a barrel, which is very rare.

---

[8] S.139 Criminal Justice Act 1988
[9] [2010] EWHC 3283 (Admin)

The crossbow was used in hunting and warfare in medieval times, being slower to reload than a longbow but requiring less strength to draw. Traditionally they were popular on the continent, the English favouring the longbow. Crossbows fell into disuse for these purposes during the 16th Century with the development of muzzle-loading firearms, but in recent decades they have been revived for target shooting purposes.

Section 1 of the Crossbows Act 1987 prohibits the sale or letting on hire of crossbows to a person under the age of 18 years. That is unless the seller believes the buyer to be over 18 and has reasonable grounds for that belief.

A person under the age of 18 must not buy or hire a crossbow. There is no provision made for test purchases by the police or trading standards in this Act, so offences would need to be founded on evidence gained by other methods or the test purchase volunteer would risk committing an unlawful act.

A person under the age of 18 must not have in his possession a crossbow that is capable of firing a missile (thus this would not apply to a deactivated crossbow) or the parts of a crossbow which, if assembled, were capable of firing a missile.

4.6     Air Weapons

Air rifles which produce muzzle energy higher than 12 foot pounds and air pistols higher than 6 foot pounds at the muzzle are classed as firearms and a firearms certificate is necessary to possess them legally. If the gun is below the stated figures then no certification of any kind is required to either buy, possess or use them. The onus is on the owner of the gun to ensure that it does not exceed those power levels. If the gun does exceed those levels, even if the owner is completely unaware of the fact, then the owner is guilty of illegal possession of a firearm.

People over the age of 18 may purchase and own low-powered air rifles and air pistols, and the ammunition for them, and also use them, but only where they have specific permission to shoot.

By section 24(1)(a) of the Firearms Act 1968, it is an offence to sell or let for hire an air weapon or ammunition for an air weapon to a person under the age of 18 years. It is also an offence to make a gift of an air weapon or ammunition for an air weapon to a person under the age of 18 years.

There is no defence of exercising reasonable precautions or exercising due diligence, making this an absolute offence if the facts are made out.

People between 14 and 17 may borrow (but not own or purchase) low-powered air rifles, air pistols and the ammunition for them, and may use them without supervision, on private premises where they have specific permission to shoot. People in this age group may not buy or hire an air rifle, air pistol or ammunition, or receive them as a gift and they may not have an air rifle or air pistol in a public place unless supervised by somebody aged 21 or over, and have a reasonable excuse to do so.

People under 14 years of age may only use low-powered air rifles and air pistols on private property where they have specific permission to shoot, and whilst they are under the direct supervision of someone 21 years of age or older. People in this age group may not buy, hire or receive an air rifle, air pistol or ammunition as a gift, or shoot, anywhere at any time, unless supervised by somebody aged 21 or over.

Air guns which make use of self-contained air or gas cartridges, where the gas or air propellant and the pellet or bullet are contained within a single self-contained cartridge, are now prohibited. (The most common example was the Brocock revolver). People who owned such airguns prior to the ban in 2004 were permitted to retain them, but only if they were entered on a firearms certificate. Even the ones held on a firearms certificate may not now be sold, or even given away. The only permitted method of disposal is to hand them to the police for destruction. Possession of such airguns without a firearms certificate carries exactly the same penalties as those for possession of other unauthorised firearms.

Since air rifles producing less than 12 foot pounds muzzle energy and air pistols producing less than 6 foot pounds of energy are not included in the firearms licensing procedures, the Firearms Acts are silent on storage requirements for such guns. However, since 10th February 2011, there is a requirement under the Crime and Security Act 2010 that airgun owners must 'take reasonable precautions to stop unauthorised access to their airguns by people under the age of 18.' The law does not specify what constitutes 'reasonable precautions' and guidance for police firearms officers says that each individual case will be dealt with on its merits and that, 'it is not possible to be prescriptive' about exact security provisions.

A person under the age of 18 must not buy or hire an air weapon. There is no provision made for test purchases by the police or trading standards in this Act, so offences would need to be founded on evidence gained by other methods or the test purchase volunteer would risk committing an unlawful act.

4.7        Firearms

The legislation on the supply of real or imitation firearms to young people is very complicated. There are restrictions for actual firearms, depending upon the type of firearm, imitation firearms that look like firearms (whether they are realistic or unrealistic) and even some firearms that are meant as toys.

Put simply, a real firearm is one that fires a projectile (bullet or shot). Ammunition includes both the projectiles (bullets and shot) capable of being fired by a real firearm and also other projectiles such as grenades or bombs, whether or not they are capable of being fired by a firearm.

From 28th July 2010 the Firearms Acts (Amendment) Regulations 2010 made a key change to the age at which a person may purchase or hire firearms, shot guns and ammunition. A person who is under 18 years of age may not purchase or hire any firearms, shot guns or ammunition. This change has been brought about by EEC Directive 2008/51/EC which harmonises the ages for purchase of firearms within the EU.

A firearm[10] is a lethal barrelled weapon of any description from which any shot, bullet or other missile can be discharged and includes:

- Any prohibited weapon, whether it is such a lethal weapon or not
- Any component part of such a lethal or prohibited weapon
- Any accessory to any such weapon designed or adapted to diminish the noise or flash caused by firing the weapon.

A shotgun is a type of firearm which is a smooth bore gun (not being an air gun) with a barrel not less than 24 inches in length and does not have a barrel with a bore greater than 2 inches. It has no shot magazine (or detachable magazine for just two shot) and is not a revolver gun[11].

By section 24(1)(b) of the Firearms Act 1968 it is an offence to sell or let on hire a firearm (including a shotgun or a powerful air weapon) or ammunition of any other description to a person under the age of 18 years.

---

[10] S.57(1) Firearms Act 1968
[11] S.1(3), Firearms Act 1968

It is also an offence to make a gift of or lend any firearm or ammunition to a person under the age of 14 years (or, if it is a shotgun or ammunition for a shotgun, 15 years).

It is a defence for the person charged to prove that the seller believed the purchaser was over the age of 18 years and that they had reasonable grounds for that belief.

There is no defence of exercising reasonable precautions or exercising due diligence, making this an absolute offence if the facts are made out.

The offence cannot be avoided by a collateral arrangement that possession of the firearm shall be retained by the seller[12].

A person under the age of 18 must not buy or hire a firearm. There is no provision made for test purchases by the police or trading standards in this Act, so offences would need to be founded on evidence gained by other methods (for instance by reference to the records of transactions[13]) or the test purchase volunteer would risk committing an unlawful act.

The Metropolitan Police have published this simplified table of the various restrictions in place:

|  | Under 18 | Under 15 | Under 14 |
|---|---|---|---|
| Purchase or hire any firearm (including shotguns and air weapons) or ammunition | No | No | No |
| Possess a Section 1 firearm and ammunition | Yes | Yes | No (see exceptions 1, 2 & 3 below) |
| Receive a Section 1 firearm and ammunition as a gift | Yes | Yes | No |
| Possess assembled shot gun and ammunition | Yes | No (see exceptions 1, 4 & 5 below) | No (see exceptions 1, 4 & 5 below) |

[12] *Watts v Seymour* [1967] 2 QB 647, [1967] 1 All ER 1044
[13] S.40(1), Firearms Act 1968

| | Under 18 | Under 15 | Under 14 |
|---|---|---|---|
| Receive a shot gun as a gift | Yes | No | No |
| Possess an air weapon | No (see exceptions 1, 2, 3, 4 & 6 below) | No (see exceptions 1,2,3, 4 & 6 below) | No (see exceptions 1,2, 3 & 4 below) |
| Receive an air weapon as a gift | No | No | No |
| Possess an air weapon in a public place | No (see exceptions 1, 2,3 & 4 below) | No (see exceptions 1, 2,3 & 4 below) | No (see exceptions 1, 2,3 & 4 below) |

**Exceptions:**

1. If carrying on behalf of the certificate holder (who is aged 18 years or over) and for the certificate holders sporting purposes only.
2. When part of an approved club or cadet corps.
3. On a miniature rifle range.
4. Under the supervision of someone over 21 years old.
5. When the shotgun is in a securely fastened gun cover so that it cannot be fired
6. Unless on private property with the permission of the land owner. It is an offence for someone under this exception to fire any missile beyond the boundary of the premises, unless with permission of the adjacent landowner

Some young shotgun and firearm certificate holders have a notice on their certificates stating that they cannot purchase shot guns until they attain the age of 17 years. This has now been increased to 18 years of age.

4.8      Ammunition, Grenades, Shot and Projectiles

Ammunition, grenades, shot and projectiles for use in firearms are also considered to be firearms and are subject to the age restrictions in place for the type of firearm in question.

Ammunition means ammunition for any firearm and includes grenades, bombs and other like missiles, whether capable of use with a firearm or not, and also prohibited ammunition. The ammunition does not have to be complete in order to be classed as such. Cartridges containing just primer are still ammunition[14].

4.9     Realistic Imitation Firearms and Unrealistic Imitation Firearms

An imitation firearm is one that resembles a real firearm[15], whether or not one that is capable of firing a projectile or being adapted to fire a projectile. It includes replica weapons and ball bearing weapons ('BB guns'). An imitation firearm is realistic if, for all practical purposes, it is indistinguishable from a real firearm. In general, it is an offence to sell realistic imitation firearms at all[16], but there are some exceptions and, where those exceptions apply, it is illegal to sell a realistic imitation firearm to a person under the age of 18 years.

The exemptions are if the supply of the realistic imitation firearm is in connection with:

- A museum or gallery
- Theatrical performances or rehearsals
- The production of films or television
- The organisation and holding of historical re-enactments
- Crown servants
- Members of softair skirmishing groups with third party liability insurance
- Members of historical re-enactment groups with third party liability insurance

An imitation firearm (but not a real firearm) is capable of being made unrealistic by making it in certain bright colours, transparent or to look like a pre-1870 revolver. These unrealistic imitation firearms (even if they are obviously intended to be toys) may not be sold to a person under the age of 18 years.

An imitation firearm is regarded as unrealistic if it is less than 38mm high and 70mm long, or if the firearm is transparent or painted bright red, bright orange, bright yellow, bright green, bright pink, bright purple or bright blue. No other colours are permitted[17].

---

[14] *R v Stubbings* [1990] Crim LR 811, CA
[15] The test is what it looked like at the time when the accused actually had it with him (see *R v Morris and King* (1984) 79 Cr App Rep 104, CA)
[16] S.36(1)(c), Violent Crime Reduction Act 2006
[17] R.6 and 7, Violent Crime Reduction Act 2006 (Realistic Imitation Firearms) Regulations 2007: SI2007:2606

4.10   Toy Guns, Water Pistols, 'Super Soakers' and Imitation 'Space Weapons'

The British Toy and Hobby Association and the Toy Retailers Association operate a joint code of practice for toy firearms.

Some 'firearms' are considered so unrealistic that they would be incapable of being considered to be imitations of anything. If they are designed or clearly intended for use in play by children under 14 years old[18], they will be regarded as a 'toy firearm'. Examples include futuristic space lasers or super soaker water pistols.

This is a question of fact and degree for magistrates to consider, so it may be risky to rely on these products being available to under 18's. However, equally, it is unlikely that Trading Standards Officers would consider it in the public interest to prosecute a retailer for selling a toy super soaker water pistol to a young person.

4.11   Licensing Controls

A person dealing in, repairing or proving firearms must have a firearms dealers certificate, which is issued by the local police force.

A certificate remains in force for three years and may be revoked or refused if:

- A court makes an order under S.45 of the Firearms Act 1968 following conviction for a firearms offence including age restricted sales offences[19]
- The chief officer of police is satisfied that he cannot be permitted to carry on business as a dealer in firearms without danger to the public safety or to the peace
- The chief officer of police is satisfied that the applicant will not engage in business as a firearms dealer to a substantial extent or as an essential part of another trade, business or profession

A purchaser of a firearm (but not an air weapon) must be the holder of either a firearms certificate or a shotgun certificate, as the case may be.

A certificate may be refused or revoked if the holder is:

---

[18] Toys (Safety) Regulations 2011 (SI2011:1881)
[19] This excludes the offence of selling an air weapon to a person under the age of 18 years (S.45 (2)(a), Firearms Act 1968)

- A danger to public safety
- Of intemperate habits
- Of unsound mind
- Unfit to be entrusted with such a firearm
- No longer has good reason for possession

## 4.12   Enforcement

Police forces have lead responsibility for firearms and offensive weapons enforcement and operating the firearms certification regime.

However, there are no specific provisions on divisions of responsibility with Trading Standards and often Trading Standards Departments will be involved in the enforcement of the age restricted sales provisions – particularly for knives and imitation firearms.

## 4.13   Penalties

The penalties for offences are expressed as maximum levels based upon the standard scale[20] applicable in Magistrates' Courts. All of the offences set out in this section are 'summary only' and may only be tried in the Magistrates' Courts.

CA1987 – Crossbows Act 1987
CJA1988 – Criminal Justice Act 1988
FA1968 – Firearms Act 1968

Level One - £200 maximum

Level Two - £500 maximum

Level Three - £1,000 maximum

S.2 – CA1987 – Purchase or hire of a crossbow by a person under 18
S.3 – CA1987 – Possession of a crossbow by a person under 18
S.22(3) – FA1968 – Person under 15 having with him a shotgun without adult supervision
S.22(4) – FA1968 – Person under 18 having with him an air weapon or

---

[20] S.37(2), Criminal Justice Act 1982 as amended by s.85 of the Legal Aid, Sentencing and Punishment of Offenders Act 2012

ammunition

S.23(1) – FA1968 – Person under 18 making improper use of air weapon when under supervision or person supervising him permitting such use

S.23(4) – FA1968 – Person under 18 making improper use of air weapon on private premises

S.24(3) – FA1968 – Making gift of shotgun to person under 15

S.24(4) – FA1968 – Supplying air weapon to person under 18


Level Four - £2,500 maximum


Level Five - unlimited fine


S.141A(1)- CJA1988 – Sale of knives to persons under 18 (note: and/or up to six months imprisonment)

S.1 – CA 1987 – Sale and letting on hire of crossbows to under 18 (note: and/or up to six months imprisonment)

S.22(1) – FA1968 – Person under 18 acquiring a firearm (note: and/or up to six months imprisonment)

S.22(1A) – FA1968 – Person under 18 using certified firearm for unauthorised purpose (note: and/or up to three months imprisonment)

S.22(2) – FA1968 – Person under 14 having firearm in his possession without lawful authority (note: and/or up to six months imprisonment)

S.24(1) – FA1968 – Selling or letting on hire a firearm to a person under 18 (note: and/or up to six months imprisonment)

S.24(2) – FA1968 – Supplying firearm or ammunition to person under 14 (note: and/or up to six months imprisonment)

S.40(5) – FA1968 – Non-compliance by firearms dealer in connection with register of transactions (note: and/or up to six months imprisonment)

CHAPTER FIVE

# LOTTERY AND GAMBLING

**CONTENTS**

5.1    Introduction

Gambling is the wager of money or money's worth on an event of uncertain outcome with the primary intent of winning more money or money's worth. Gambling is strictly regulated in the UK, covering gaming, betting and participation in lotteries. Gaming is playing a game of chance for a prize. Betting is placing a stake on the outcome of a race, competition, event or other process; the likelihood of something occurring or not; or whether or not something is true. Lotteries are where a person pays to participate and where prizes are allocated purely by chance.

5.2    Key Legislation

Gambling Act 2005
National Lottery Act 1993

5.3    Summary of Age Restricted Laws relating to Lotteries and Gambling

- It is an offence, subject to some exceptions, to invite, cause or permit a child (under 16) or a young person (16-18) to gamble
- It is an offence to invite or permit a child (under 16) or a young person (16-18) to enter a casino or a betting premises (other than a track)
- It is an offence to invite or permit a child (under 16) or a young person (16-18) to enter an adult gaming centre or a part of a family entertainment centre that contains category C gaming machines
- A young person (meaning someone aged 16 – 18) commits an offence if he enters a restricted area or, subject to some exceptions, if he gambles or provides facilities for gambling. There is no similar offence for a child (under 16)
- It is an offence, subject to some exceptions, to invite, cause or permit a child (under 16) to participate in a lottery (excluding the National Lottery, which is considered below)
- It is an offence to invite, cause or permit a child (under 16) to participate in the football pools
- There are also restrictions on the employment of children and young people in the gambling industry, but that is outside the scope of this book
- It is a defence for the person charged to prove that he took all reasonable

steps to determine the individuals age and that he reasonably believed the individual was not a child or young person

- It is an offence to sell a National Lottery ticket to a person who has not attained the age of 16 years

## 5.4   The National Lottery

The National Lottery is governed by specific legislation, which is enforced by the lottery operator in the UK, Camelot plc. It is also occasionally enforced by local Trading Standards Departments.

By regulation 1 of the National Lottery Regulations 1994, it is illegal for a National Lottery ticket to be sold by or to a person under the age of 16 years.

A National Lottery ticket includes any prize draw operated by or through the National Lottery Operator (including the main *Lotto* draw, *Thunderball*, *EuroMillions Draw*, etc) and any scratch cards issued by or through the National Lottery Operator.

There is no defence of exercising reasonable precautions or exercising due diligence, however, the courts have held that this is an offence of strict liability[1].

In practice, this legislation is enforced by Camelot under Operation Child. A test purchase failure will usually result in a warning letter and a further test purchase attempt. A second failure may result in the revocation of the lottery terminal in the retailer. That is often penalty in itself, so there have been relatively few prosecutions before the court.

It is also worth noting that Camelot has acted to remove lottery terminals from retailers that have been convicted of selling other age restricted products to children. This can, for instance, be an indirect consequence of the suspension of an alcohol licence by a local authority for under age sales.

## 5.5   Other Lotteries

From 1st September 2007, the Gambling Act 2005 introduced a new licensing and enforcement regime for lotteries other than the National Lottery.

A 'lottery' is where persons are required to pay in order to take part in an

---

[1] *London Borough of Harrow v Dilip Shah and Anor* [1999] EWHC Admin 319

arrangement, during the course of which one or more prizes are allocated by a process which relies wholly on chance, unless it is an exempt lottery[2].

There are two broad categories of lottery operator:

- An operator with annual sales of less than £250,000 or with proceeds in a single lottery of less than £20,000 are local lotteries and require registration with their local Licensing Authority
- An operator with annual sales of more than £250,000 or with proceeds in a single lottery in excess of £20,000 are large lotteries and require registration with the Gambling Commission

A minimum of 20% of the proceeds of a lottery must be paid to the 'good cause' they are promoting; the remainder may be used for prizes and reasonable expenses.

By section 56(1) of the Gambling Act 2005, it is illegal to invite, cause or permit any person under the age of 16 to participate in a lottery (unless it is an exempt lottery).

It is a statutory condition[3] applied to the licence of all lottery operators that if the licensee becomes aware that a child is using or has used the lottery, the licensee:

- Must return any money paid (whether by way of fee, stake or otherwise) by the child as soon as reasonably practicable and
- May not give a prize to the child

The Gambling Commission promotes a statutory code of practice for lottery operators. This requires that licensees must have and put into effect policies and procedures designed to minimise the risk of lottery tickets being sold to children. This must include procedures for:

- Checking the age of apparently under age purchasers of lottery tickets
- Taking action when there are unlawful attempts to purchase tickets

From 8 May 2015, amendments to the statutory licence conditions and codes

---

[2] Certain non-commercial lotteries are exempt, subject to strict conditions, see Schedule 11, Gambling Act 2005
[3] S.83(1) Gambling Act 2005, it is an offence to fail to comply with this condition, s. 58, Gambling Act 2005

of practice mean that it must be clear in the terms and conditions that those under 16 are not permitted to participate and prizes will not be paid out. Customers must be required to verify their age before being able to make any subscription or purchase entry into the lottery.

The operator is expected to conduct random checks of users who self-verify age.

In addition the ordinary code provisions (which are effectively guidance and best practice) state that where the lottery is more likely to attract underage play, eg prizes that appeal to children, operators should ensure age verification measures are appropriate to the risk of attempted underage play.

Licensees must take all reasonable steps to ensure that all those engaged in the promotion of lotteries in reliance on the licence understand their responsibilities for preventing under age gambling, returning stakes and not paying prizes to under age customers (see chapter ten, *post*).

5.6      The Football Pools

The football pools are a betting pool based on predicting the outcome of top-level association football (often covering the English and Scottish Football Association matches) set to take place in the coming week.

By section 57 (1) of the Gambling Act 2005, it is illegal to invite, cause or permit a person under the age of 16 years to participate in the football pools.

Inviting a child to participate in the football pools includes, in particular, intentionally sending a child (under 16) any document which advertises the pools or bringing to their attention information about the pools with a view to encouraging them to participate. This also applies to any person named on the document as being a person to whom payment can be made or information obtained, or any advertiser of the lottery unless that person can prove that the document was sent to the child without his authority and consent.

5.7      Access to Gambling Premises

The Gambling Act 2005 is split into general offences relating to a 'child' aged under 16 years and a 'young person' aged 16 to 18 years. Many of the offences can also be committed by young people engaging in gambling activities, but cannot be committed by a child. The Act covers sales, gambling participation and access involving children and young people. It also regulates the employment of children and young people by gambling providers, but that is outside the scope of this book.

By section 47 it is illegal to invite or permit a person under the age of 18 years to enter a casino, betting premises, adult gaming centre or certain parts of a race track.

By section 47 (7), it is illegal to invite or permit a person under the age of 18 years to enter an area within a family entertainment centre that contains any category C gaming machines that are available for use (that is a machine with a minimum stake of £1 and a maximum prize of £100).

It is a defence to show that you took all reasonable steps to determine the child or young person's age and that you reasonably believed them to be over the relevant age. There is no defence of exercising reasonable precautions or exercising due diligence, making this an absolute offence if the facts are made out (see chapter ten, *post*).

It should be noted that these offences apply not only to the owners and operators of the gambling premises, but also to any other person including the parent, guardian or any other adult responsible for the child or young person.

Children and young people are not permitted into a gambling premise even if they are accompanied by an adult who is participating in gambling. There is no lower limit for this absolute prohibition so, for instance, a baby in a pushchair or a babe-in-arms could not be brought into a betting shop whilst their parent places a bet, even though there is no likelihood that the child would participate in gambling.

## 5.8      Gambling

By section 48 (1) it is illegal for a person aged 16 years to 18 years to gamble (subject to some exceptions, such as the football pools) or to enter any casino, betting premises, adult gaming centre and certain parts of race tracks or family entertainment centres. A child (under 16) does not commit an offence if they gamble, but the gambling provider would.

It is also illegal for a person aged 16 years to 18 years to enter premises in circumstances where a person would commit an offence if he invited or permitted the young person to enter. However, this would not apply to the use

---

[4] S.83(1) Gambling Act 2005, it is an offence to fail to comply with this condition, S.58, Gambling Act 2005

of young people in enforcement operations (see section 5.11, *post*).

There is no defence available to young people who commit these offences, making them absolute offences if the facts are made out.

By section 46 (1) of the Gambling Act 2005, it is illegal to invite, cause or permit any person under the age of 16 to participate in any gambling activity (subject to some exceptions).

The Gambling Commission issue individual licences for each type of gambling activity and they all have a statutory condition[4] applied to the licence that if the licensee becomes aware that a child or young person is using or participating in gambling, the licensee:

- Must return any money paid (whether by way of fee, stake or otherwise) by the child as soon as reasonably practicable and
- May not give a prize to the child

Gambling providers are also required to have and put into effect policies and procedures designed to minimise the risk of illegal gambling by children and young people. This must include procedures for:

- Checking the age of apparently under age participants in gambling
- Taking action when there are unlawful attempts to participate in underage gambling

From 8 May 2015, gambling providers need to put into place strengthened social responsibility provisions as a result of an update to the statutory Licence Conditions and Codes of Practice (LCCP).

These include statutory licence conditions for:

- a requirement for casinos and larger operators to conduct test purchasing, as a means of monitoring the effectiveness of their policies and procedures designed to prevent underage gambling
- improved training, policies, procedures and control measures to ensure access to gambling by children and young people is prevented

Social responsibility code provisions (which have the effect of statutory licence conditions) to:

- ensure that their policies and procedures take account of the structure and layout of their gambling premises to prevent access to gambling by children and young persons

- ensure staff training covers all relevant prohibitions against inviting children or young persons to gamble or to enter gambling premises
- conduct test purchasing or take part in collective test purchasing programmes to provide reasonable assurance that they have effective policies and procedures to prevent underage gambling. Test purchase results should be provided to the Commission.

Additional ordinary code provisions (which are effectively best practice guidelines) state that:

- Licensees should consider how they monitor the effectiveness of their policies and procedures for preventing underage gambling, for example through collective test purchasing programmes, and be able to explain their approach.
- Staff training on preventing underage gambling should include policies for induction and refresher training.

Licensees must take all reasonable steps to ensure that all those engaged in the promotion of gambling in reliance on the licence understand their responsibilities for preventing under age gambling, returning stakes and not paying prizes to under age customers (see chapter ten, *post*).

5.9      Using Gaming Machines

Gaming machines provide games of chance where the prizes awarded are in money or money's worth. Gaming machines, commonly known as fruit machines, are often reel-based, though increasingly use advanced software and digital displays. Gaming machines must be a game of chance, not a game of skill, such as a quiz machine.

There are complex rules and categories for the placement, number, stakes and prizes for gaming machines. Those rules are outside the scope of this book.

However, since July 2011, it is illegal for any person aged under 18 years to use any gaming machine with a minimum stake of £1 or more and a maximum cash prize of £100 or more. These are category A, B & C gaming machines.

It is not illegal for a child or young person to use:

- A machine with a maximum stake of 30p and a non-money prize not exceeding £8 in value

- A crane grab machine with a maximum stake of £1 and a non-money prize not exceeding £50 in value
- A machine with a maximum stake of 10p and a cash prize not exceeding £5
- A combined money and non-money prize machine (other than a coin pusher or penny falls machine) with a maximum stake of 10p and a maximum prize of £8 (of which no more than £5 may be in cash)
- A combined money and non-money prize machine (coin pusher or penny falls machine) with a maximum stake of 20p and a maximum prize of £20 (of which no more than £10 may be in cash)

These are category D gaming machines.

In section 59, the Secretary of State can bring in regulations placing age restrictions on these machines, but no regulations have thus far been enacted.

## 5.10   Licensing Controls

### 5.10.1   Gambling Commission Licensing

Licences for gambling operators, facilities, 'remote gambling', the football pools or large lotteries are issued by the Gambling Commission.

In addition to the general conditions on licences described above, by section 77 the Gambling Commission may impose specific conditions on individual licences, such as those that have been found to have breached the under age gambling provisions.

The Commission has extensive powers to impose conditions on individual licences, including, but not limited to:

- Requiring licences to limit or restrict their activities
- Requiring licences to employ more staff, change the layout of premises, devote more financial resources to management of the premises
- Restricting the methods of communication that may be used promoting the business
- Making provision about establishing the identity of participants, keeping records of identity or requiring advance registration of participants

A review of a licence may be commenced under S.116, but only by the Commission. A review of a licence can result in revocation, suspension, amendment or the imposition of a financial penalty (only in the event a licence condition is breached). The Commission regularly takes enforcement action under these provisions and publishes the details of them on their website.

Appeal lies to the First Tier Tribunal (General Regulatory Chamber).

### 5.10.2   Local Authority Licensing

Small lotteries registrations and licences for most gambling premises are issued by the local Licensing Authority.

A review of a licence may be commenced under S.197 of the Gambling Act 2005 by a responsible body which includes (but is not limited to) the Commission, the local Licensing Authority, the local police and the local Safeguarding Children Board. A review of a licence can result in revocation, suspension or amendment, but there are no financial penalty provisions for local Licensing Authorities.

Appeal lies to the local Magistrates' Court.

### 5.10.3   National Lottery Operator – Terminal Licence Arrangements

The National Lottery Operator, currently Camelot plc, maintain arrangements for providing lottery terminals in retail premises and scratch cards. This is a contractual arrangement between the National Lottery Operator and individual retailers. The terminal licence can be revoked under the terms of that contract.

### 5.11   Enforcement

Enforcement is generally undertaken by the Gambling Commission.

Theoretically, a local Licensing Authority is empowered under section 64 to undertake test purchase operations, but they are not empowered by section 346 of the Act to prosecute for any under age offences, so it is difficult to see why they would lead on such operations. In practice, they coordinate and cooperate with the Gambling Commission on enforcement.

There are no powers for Trading Standards Officers in this Act unless they are delegated powers by the local Licensing Authority, which in unitary authority areas, will be the same local authority.

Police officers have powers under section 64 to undertake test purchase operations and may report offences to the Crown Prosecution Service to institute proceedings. However, in practice, they coordinate and cooperate with the Gambling Commission on enforcement.

Enforcement for the National Lottery is generally undertaken by the operator, Camelot plc. However, occasional enforcement is also undertaken by local Trading Standards Departments.

5.12    Penalties

The penalties for offences are expressed as maximum levels based upon the standard scale[5] applicable in Magistrates' Courts. Most of the offences set out in this section are 'summary only' and may only be tried in the Magistrates' Courts. Uniquely, in under age sales enforcement an offence under the National Lotteries Act 1993 can be tried on indictment in the Crown Court and on conviction could attract an unlimited fine and/or a prison sentence up to two years.

GA2005 – Gambling Act 2005
NLA1993 – National Lotteries Act 1993

Level One - £200 maximum

Level Two - £500 maximum

Level Three - £1,000 maximum

S.48(1) – GA2005 – Young person (16-18) gambling
S.49 – GA2005 – Young person (16-18) entering restricted gambling premises

Level Four - £2,500 maximum

Level Five - unlimited fine

S.46(1) – GA2005 – Causing, permitting inviting a child or young person to gamble (note: and/or up to six months imprisonment)
S.47(1) – GA2005 – Inviting or permitting a child or young person on a casino premises (note: and/or up to six months imprisonment)
S.47(4) – GA2005 – Inviting or permitting a child or young person on a betting

---

[5] S.37(2), Criminal Justice Act 1982  as amended by s.85 of the Legal Aid, Sentencing and Punishment of Offenders Act 2012

premises (note: and/or up to six months imprisonment)

S.47(5) – GA2005 – Inviting or permitting a child or young person in an adult gaming centre (note: and/or up to six months imprisonment)

S.47(6) – GA2005 – Inviting or permitting a child or young person in certain track areas (note: and/or up to six months imprisonment)

S.47(7) – GA2005 – Inviting or permitting a child or young person in an area of a family entertainment centre with a category C gaming machine (note: and/or up to six months imprisonment)

S.56(1) – GA2005 – Inviting or permitting a child to participate in a lottery (note: and/or up to six months imprisonment)

S.57(1) – GA2005 – Inviting or permitting a child to participate in the football pools (note: and/or up to six months imprisonment)

S.13(1) – NLA1993 – Breach of National Lottery Licensing Conditions (note: and/or up to six months imprisonment – and potential for trial on indictment or referral to the Crown Court for an unlimited fine and/or up to two years imprisonment)

CHAPTER SIX

# SOLVENTS, AEROSOL PRODUCTS & PETROLEUM

## CONTENTS

6.1      Introduction

Volatile substance abuse is the deliberate inhaling of volatile substances to achieve intoxication. It is commonly referred to as 'glue sniffing', 'buzzing gas' or 'tooting'. According to the Department of Health[1], it is responsible for more deaths in children and young people than illegal drugs. Around 60 – 75 people die every year from volatile substance abuse.

6.2      Key Legislation

Intoxicating Substances (Supply) Act 1985
Cigarette Lighter Refills (Safety) Regulations 1999
Anti-Social Behaviour Act 2003
Petroleum (Consolidation) Regulations 2014

6.3      Summary of Age Restricted Laws relating to Solvents, Aerosol Products and Petroleum

- It is an offence to supply or offer to supply a substance (other than a controlled drug) to a person under the age of 18 if he knows or has reasonable cause to believe that the substance (or its fumes) is likely to be inhaled by the person for the purpose of causing intoxication
- It is an offence to supply any cigarette lighter refill canister containing butane to any person under the age of 18 years
- It is an offence to sell an aerosol paint container to a person under the age of 16 years
- It is an offence for a person aged under 16 to use petrol dispensing equipment and it is an offence to supply or allow the supply of petrol to a person aged under 16

6.4      Solvents and Volatile Organic Compounds

The Intoxicating Substances (Supply) Act 1985 was introduced to tackle the growing trend of young people using strong glues and butane gases to intoxicate themselves.

---

[1] Department of Health: *'Out of Sight? ... not out of mind' – A Framework for Volatile Substance Abuse* 2005

By section 1, it is illegal for any person to sell any substance to any person under the age of 18 years if he has reasonable cause to believe them to be under 18 and he has reasonable grounds to believe the substance will be used by that person to cause intoxication. This does not apply to controlled drugs as they are covered by the Misuse of Drugs Act 1971.

There is a similar offence for supplying substances to others that the seller knows or has reason to believe will be used by a person under the age of 18 years to cause intoxication. This is known as 'proxy sales'.

The offence is considered difficult to enforce because of the requisite knowledge that the purchaser will use the product to cause intoxication. Although test purchasing can be used to identify poor practice, it cannot form the basis of a criminal charge because, obviously, the test purchaser would not use the product for self-intoxication and the retailer would have no reason to believe that they would.

It is a defence for a person under the age of 18 years to show that they supplied the substance otherwise than in the course of a business. As this is an offence that requires knowledge on the part of the seller, there is no defence of taking reasonable precautions and exercising due diligence available.

In practice, formal enforcement action for this offence has been rare and, since the introduction of stricter controls on butane lighter refills (see section 6.6, *post*) enforcement has tended to concentrate on them.

Nevertheless, retailers ought to include any products that can be inhaled to cause intoxication on their list of age restricted products. Examples include:

- Cyanoacrylate (super glue)
- Polyvinyl acetate (PVA) glues
- Correcting fluid
- Oven cleaners
- Acetone (commonly found in nail polish remover)
- Aerosols
- Pain relief sprays
- Paint stripper
- Anti-freeze
- Marker pens (particularly those containing toluene or xylene, such as permanent markers)
- Horse or animal liniments
- Dry cleaning fluid

There are some common misconceptions about the scope of this restriction. The product has to be, at least, capable of causing intoxication if inhaled. Products like solid glue sticks, adhesive putty, pressure sensitive tape (such as 'sticky tape') and self-sealing envelopes, whilst containing glue are not capable of causing intoxication and are, therefore, not caught by these provisions. The legislation does not prohibit supplying solvents to persons under the age of 18 for their normal intended use.

Retailers are urged to look out for obvious signs of abuse, such as the smell of glue or solvents on the person's clothes, slurred speech and behaviour similar to drunkenness, or spots and sores around the mouth and nose. In addition, retailers should be suspicious if a purchaser is frequently buying solvents or is buying solvents and plastic bags together.

6.5    New Psychoactive Substances

The government has been conducting a review of legislation surrounding new psychoactive substances, more commonly referred to as 'legal highs', 'designer drugs' and 'club drugs'. Some substances described as 'legal highs' may not actually be legal (and 'legal' can imply they are safe or regulated, when neither is true). In 2013-14, nearly a fifth (19%) of the substances found in the 'legal high' drug samples collected by the Home Office's forensic early warning system in 2013-14 were controlled drugs.

Some New Psychoactive Substances may have been legally available when first introduced but are now controlled under the Misuse of Drugs Act. These include mephedrone, 2-DPMP (sold as ivory wave) and some synthetic cannabinoids (often called spice).

There are no specific laws to prohibit New Psychoactive Substances, but on occasion, local Trading Standards Officers have used the Intoxicating Substances (Supply) Act 1985 (see section 6.4, ante). On 29th May 2015 the government published the New Psychoactive Substances Bill which aims to ban all of these 'legal highs'.

6.6    Butane Lighter Refills

From October 1999, following recognition of the limitations of the Intoxicating Substances (Supply) Act 1985, the Cigarette Lighter Refill (Safety) Regulations 1999 were introduced. This effectively removed the requirement for the retailer to know or have reason to believe that cigarette lighter refills would be used for intoxication.

By regulation 2, it is illegal to supply a cigarette lighter refill canister containing butane to any person under the age of 18 years.

It is also illegal to supply any substance containing butane to any person under the age of 18 years. It should be noted that, although the title of the regulations refers to 'cigarette lighter refills', this provision is also considered to cover other butane gas cylinders, such as cartridges for camping stoves, caravans or barbeque lighting sticks.

It is a defence for a person supplying cigarette lighter refills or substances containing butane to show that they took all reasonable precautions and exercised all due diligence to avoid selling them to persons under the age of 18 years (see chapter ten, *post*).

6.7    Household Chemicals

There is a common misconception that many household chemicals, such as bleach, cleaning fluid, or shoe polish, are age restricted products.

However, many retailers place voluntary restrictions on items like bleach, cleaning fluids, dishwasher tablets, washing powder and shoe polish. This is perfectly lawful (see section 9.15, *post*).

6.8    Spray Paint

The use of spray paint has caused problems for communities and property owners by the proliferation of graffiti. In 2003, as part of a clamp down on anti-social behaviour, the government banned the supply of spray paints to persons under 16.

The legislation is contained within the Anti-Social Behaviour Act 2003.

Under section 54, it is an offence to sell an aerosol paint container to a person under the age of 16. Aerosol paint containers are defined in subsection 2 and mean a device which contains paint stored under pressure, designed to permit the release of the paint as a spray. It only includes paint in the normal sense of the word, i.e. coloured liquids used for decorating and not items such as glitter sprays which are called paint, but are not really paint at all. Also, 'paint' used to colour hair is not paint within its normal definition.

---

[2] In a letter to the Local Government Association, 14th December 2004

The Home Office has further stated[2] that it considers paint to be something that causes permanent colouration, rather than temporary Christmas spray decorations or 'silly string'.

The offence may be committed by the business or those who work on the premises, whether paid or unpaid, in a capacity that gives them the authority to prevent the sale.

It is a defence for the person who supplied the paint to show that they took steps to verify the age of the purchaser and that he reasonably believed the person to be over 16 years of age.

It is a defence for a person who employs the person that supplied the paint to show that they took all reasonable precautions and exercised all due diligence to avoid selling the paint to persons under 16 years of age (see chapter ten, *post*)

6.9    Petroleum Spirit

By Regulation 12(2) of the Petroleum (Consolidation) Regulations 2014 it is an offence for person under 16 years of age to operate a petroleum dispenser on dispensing premises.

It is also an offence for a person to supply or allow the supply of petrol to a person under 16 years of age.

Petrol means petroleum or a mixture of petroleum with one or more substances which—

(a) is liquid or viscous at a temperature of 15°C and a pressure of 101.325 kPa (1013.25 mb); and

(b) when tested in accordance with Part A.9 of the Annex to Council Regulation (EC) No 440/2008 (laying down the test methods pursuant to Regulation (EC) No 1907/2006 of the European Parliament and of the Council on the Registration, Evaluation, Authorisation and Restriction of Chemicals REACH), has a flash point (as defined in that Part) of less than 21°C;

So this definition would exclude diesel oil which typically has a flash point between 52 & 95 °C.

These provisions are enforced by the Petroleum Licensing Authority, which may be the local fire and rescue service, trading standards or environmental health department. The Authority issues petroleum certificates which replace the former licensing regime.

6.10     Licensing Controls

There are no relevant licensing controls for retailers of solvents or cigarette lighter refills.

Petroleum Certificates are issued by local Petroleum Licensing Authority, which is usually the local trading standards or environmental health authority or (in London or the Metropolitan Counties of England) the local fire and rescue service.

6.11     Enforcement

Section 27 (1) of the Consumer Protection Act 1987 places a duty on the local weights and measures authority (Trading Standards Department) to enforce safety provisions within their area. This includes the provisions on the sale of cigarette lighter refills.

Unlike most under age sales legislation, enforcement officers have extensive powers of investigation for breaches of the cigarette lighter refills regulations. In particular, powers to enter and inspect premises, seize and detain documents, seize and detain goods and records and undertake test purchases. The detail of these powers is not within the scope of this book.

There is no duty on local authorities to *enforce* the restrictions on spray paints, but by section 54A[3] of the Anti-Social Behaviour Act 2003 every year local authorities are required to consider the extent to which it is appropriate to carry out a programme of enforcement action in their area, and to carry out such a programme.

The programme of action can include bringing prosecutions, investigating complaints or taking other measures to reduce the incidence of under age sales of spray paint.

There are no specific duties of enforcement under the Intoxicating Substances (Supply) Act 1985. However, these offences are usually enforced by the local Trading Standards Department.

---

[3] Added by S.32 Clean Neighbourhoods and Environment Act 2005

The local Petroleum Licensing Authority is the enforcing authority within its area for petroleum certificates.

6.12      Penalties

The penalties for offences are expressed as maximum levels based upon the standard scale[4] applicable in Magistrates' Courts. All of the offences set out in this section are 'summary only' and may only be tried in the Magistrates' Courts.

ASB2003 – Anti-Social Behaviour Act 2003
CPA1987 – Consumer Protection Act 1987
ISSA1987 – Intoxicating Substances (Supply) Act 1985
PCR2014 – Petroleum (Consolidation) Regulations 2014

Level One - £200 maximum

Level Two - £500 maximum

Level Three - £1,000 maximum

Level Four - £2,500 maximum

S.54(1) – ASB2003 – Supply of aerosol paint to under 16 years

Level Five - unlimited fine

S.12(1) – CPA1987 – Breach of a safety regulation (note: and/or up to six months imprisonment)
S.1(1) – ISSA1985 – Supply of intoxicating substance to a person under 18 (note: and/or up to six months imprisonment)
R.12(2) - PCR2014 - Supply of petrol to a person aged under 16

---

[4] S.37(2), Criminal Justice Act 1982 as amended by s.85 of the Legal Aid, Sentencing and Punishment of Offenders Act 2012

CHAPTER SEVEN

# FIREWORKS AND EXPLOSIVES

## CONTENTS

## 7.1 Introduction

The safety of fireworks is always a widely discussed topic around Guy Fawkes Night on the 5th November each year. There have been sustained calls for them to be banned from sale to the general public, but thus far politicians have resisted this. Instead, extensive controls on the manufacture, transportation, storage and supply of fireworks have been introduced, including age restrictions.

Fireworks are explosives and they can and do cause significant injuries if misused. The most common injuries are burns from hand-held fireworks such as sparklers, or failing to properly follow the product instructions. There are also injuries due to people being hit by projectiles fired from fireworks, although these can usually be explained by people setting up fireworks incorrectly. The government and local authorities usually run a Firework Safety Campaign in October and November each year and have developed a firework code for people using or storing fireworks.

## 7.2 Key Legislation

Consumer Protection Act 1987
Explosives Act 1875
Fireworks Act 2003
Fireworks Regulations 2004
Pyrotechnic Articles (Safety) Regulations 2010

## 7.3 Summary of Age Restricted Laws relating to Fireworks and Explosives

- It is illegal to sell adult fireworks to any person under the age of 18 years
- It is illegal to sell party poppers, serpents, Christmas crackers and novelty matches to any person under the age of 16 years
- It is illegal for a person under the age of 18 years to possess a firework in a public place (which effectively also prohibits them from purchasing fireworks)
- However, a test purchase volunteer purchasing fireworks on behalf of a local authority would be exempt from the possession offence
- It is illegal to sell gunpowder to any person under the age of 16 years

- It is illegal to supply category 2 or 3 fireworks that have been removed from a selection or primary pack that was intended for supply as a single unit

## 7.4   Fireworks

Fireworks are a type of pyrotechnic article that contain explosive substances designed to produce heat, light, sound, gas or smoke through a self-sustained exothermic chemical reaction. They are intended for entertainment and are popular in the UK, particularly around the celebration of Guy Fawkes Night on the 5th November each year.

Fireworks, like firearms, are age restricted products where the minimum restrictions are set at European level[1]. Although a harmonisation measure, Article 6.2 of the Directive does not preclude measures taken by a Member State to prohibit or restrict the possession, use and/or the sale to the general public [of pyrotechnic articles], which are justified on the grounds of public order, security or safety, or environmental protection.

Pyrotechnic articles are categorised as follows[2]:
In relation to fireworks:

- Category 1 is a category of fireworks which present a very low hazard and negligible noise level and which are intended for use in confined areas, including fireworks which are intended for use inside domestic buildings (examples include Christmas crackers, party poppers, novelty matches, throw downs, serpents and cracker snaps)
- Category 2 is a category of fireworks which present a low hazard and low noise level and which are intended for outdoor use in confined areas (examples include garden fireworks, battery shot tubes and most fireworks with a debris scatter radius of less than 3m)
- Category 3 is a category of fireworks which present a medium hazard, which are intended for outdoor use in large open areas and whose noise level is not harmful to human health (examples include open space fireworks, rockets and most fireworks with a debris scatter radius of less than 20m)
- Category 4 is a category of fireworks which present a high hazard, which are intended for outdoor use only by persons with specialist knowledge (commonly known as fireworks for professional use) and whose noise level is not harmful to human health

---

[1] Directive 2007/23/EC on the placing on the market of pyrotechnic articles
[2] Schedule 1, Pyrotechnic Articles (Safety) Regulations 2010

In relation to theatrical pyrotechnic articles:

- Category T1 is a category of pyrotechnical articles for stage use which present a low hazard
- Category T2 is a category of pyrotechnical articles for stage use which are intended for use only by persons with specialist knowledge

In relation to other pyrotechnical articles:

- Category P1 is a category of pyrotechnical articles, other than fireworks or theatrical pyrotechnics, which present a low hazard
- Category P2 is a category of pyrotechnical articles, other than fireworks or theatrical pyrotechnics, which are intended for use only by persons with specialist knowledge

Article 7.1 of the Directive lays down specific age limits for sales of certain categories of pyrotechnic articles. By Article 7.2, the age limits are the minimum ages that may be set by Member States, higher age limits may be set on the grounds of public order, security or safety.

The minimum age limits set at EU level are:
Category 1 – 12 years
Category 2 – 16 years
Category T1 & P1 – 18 years
There are no minimum age limits set in the Directive for category 3, 4, T2 or P2 pyrotechnics.

After undertaking a consultation exercise, the UK government decided to retain the pre-existing age restrictions as:
Category 1 – 16 years
Category 2 – 18 years
Category 3 – 18 years
Category 4 – Only available to persons with specialist knowledge
Category T1 – 18 years
Category T2 – Only available to persons with specialist knowledge
Category P1 – 18 years
Category P2 – Only available to persons with specialist knowledge

However, as a result of the Red Tape Review (see section 1.3, *ante*), the restrictions on Christmas crackers have been reduced to the EU minimum of 12 years.

The Pyrotechnic Articles (Safety) Regulations 2010[3] implement the Directive in the UK.

All category 1, 2 or 3 fireworks are required by regulation 14 (3) to be labelled in English, with, among other things, the category of firework and the minimum age limit that applies to the sale of that firework in the UK.

By virtue of Regulation 15 (2) no person shall supply a category 2 or 3 firework to any person aged under 18 years.

It is a defence for a person supplying fireworks to show that they took all reasonable precautions and exercised all due diligence to avoid selling them to persons under the age of 18 years (see chapter ten, *post*).

Certain types of category 2 or 3 fireworks are banned altogether, unless it is to an authorised person with specialist knowledge, these include:

- An aerial wheel
- A banger, flash banger or double banger
- A jumping cracker
- A jumping around spinner
- A spinner
- A mini rocket
- A shot tube (such as an air bomb or shell-in-mortar)
- A battery containing bangers, flash bangers or double bangers
- A combination (other than a wheel) which includes one or more bangers, flash bangers or double bangers

All of the above fireworks, certain theatrical pyrotechnics, all category 4 fireworks and some other pyrotechnics are not permitted to be sold to the general public, only to a person with specialist knowledge. By virtue of Regulation 42, persons with specialist knowledge are required to have received appropriate training, have experience of using these fireworks and have valid specialist third party insurance for professional pyro technicians. This insurance also usually requires them to be over 18 years and may set a higher age requirement, depending upon the assessment of risks by the insurance company.

By virtue of Regulation 33 (2) no person shall supply a category T1 theatrical

---

[3] SI2010:1554

pyrotechnic article or a category P1 other pyrotechnic article firework to any person aged under 18 years.

7.5     Party Poppers, Serpents, Caps and Novelty Matches

Party poppers, serpents, caps, Christmas crackers, throw downs and novelty matches are category 1 fireworks. Whilst they are generally quite safe, they can be a nuisance if misused, particularly for animals.

Regulation 15 (2) states that no person shall supply a category 1 firework to any person aged under 16 years.

From 6th April 2013, the law relating to category 1 fireworks was changed so that Christmas crackers may not be sold to any person aged under 12 years. The restrictions for other category 1 fireworks remained unchanged.[4]

It is a defence for a person supplying fireworks to show that they took all reasonable precautions and exercised all due diligence to avoid selling them to persons under the age of 16 years (see chapter ten, *post*).

Percussion caps intended specifically for toys are excluded from the Pyrotechnic Articles (Safety) Regulations 2010 and, therefore, from 4th July 2010, they ceased to be an age restricted product. In order to be regarded as a percussion cap, they must be small discs, single caps or roll caps of shock-sensitive explosive compounds that provide noise and smoke, specifically in toy guns. Percussion caps for real or imitation firearms, or firearms that are not intended to be toys, remain category 1 fireworks and thus cannot be sold to any person under 16 years. Examples might include percussion caps for use in historical re-enactments or in theatrical, film or television productions.

7.6     Sparklers

A sparkler is a rigid wire article partially coated along one end with slow-burning pyrotechnic composition, with or without an ignition head and designed to be held in the hand. The principal effect is to emit sparks, with or without aural effects (other than a report).

Sparklers are usually category 2 fireworks and, therefore, cannot be sold to any

---

[4] By the Product Safety Amendment and Revocation Regulations 2012 (SI2012:2963): for the definition of 'Christmas Cracker' see p.211, *post*.

person under 18 years. However, they are often given to children to use, so are required to contain a specific warning.

By Regulation 14 (7) the packet in which a sparkler is contained shall include the words:

>'*Warning: not to be given to children under 5 years of age*'

No alternate words are permitted.

7.7     Mandatory Warning Notices

By Regulation 10 (1) of the Fireworks Regulations 2004, any person who exposes adult fireworks for supply must display a mandatory warning notice.

The notice must be displayed in a prominent position in the premises, or where the sale is otherwise than in a premises (such as on the internet), the information must be given to the person to whom the fireworks are supplied or exposed for supply.

The notice must state:

>'*It is illegal to sell adult fireworks or sparklers to anyone under the age of 18*'

>'*It is illegal for anyone under the age of 18 to possess adult fireworks in a public place*'

No alternate forms of words are permitted. The notice must be not less than 400mm by 300mm (slightly smaller than A3 size paper) and the characters shall not be less than 16mm high.

Adult fireworks include all categories of firework (except category 1), so this notice is required to be displayed in premises retailing category 2 or 3 fireworks to the general public and in premises retailing other fireworks only to persons with specialist knowledge and training (professional fireworks).

If the business is mail order or on the internet, the required information must be provided to each visitor of the website or reader of the catalogue. There are no requirements about prominence or size in these circumstances, but it is recommended for websites that the information appear on the homepage for the products and be provided during the checkout process for order confirmation, with a check box for the reader to tick that they have read and understood the warning (for more information about internet sales of age restricted goods, see section 10.11, *post*).

It is a defence for the person charged to prove that he took all reasonable precautions and exercised all due diligence to avoid the commission of the offence (see chapter ten, *post*).

## 7.8    Gunpowder

Not all explosives are in the form of fireworks and the old offence prohibiting the supply of gunpowder to children remains on the statute books. However, it is now largely redundant as a result of the Pyrotechnic Articles (Safety) Regulations 2010.

By section 31 of the Explosives Act 1875, gunpowder shall not be sold to any person apparently under the age of 16 years.

From 4th July 2010, this provision no longer applied to any category 1, 2 or 3 fireworks or percussion caps. From 4th July 2013 the provision ceased to apply to category 4, category T1 or T2 theatrical pyrotechnic articles or category P1 or P2 pyrotechnic articles.

Now the section only applies to pure gunpowder or any article containing gunpowder that is not a firework, pyrotechnic article, percussion cap or ammunition. It is difficult to envisage anything that this would cover, but theoretically it could include things like fuse wire containing gunpowder.

## 7.9    Licensing Controls

A retailer of fireworks, as a keeper of explosives, must hold a licence issued by their local Explosives Licensing Authority[5] (which may be the local Trading Standards Department, Licensing Authority or Fire and Rescue Authority depending upon local arrangements).

The general rules on explosives registrations will be sufficient for the safe storage of most category 1, 2 and 3 fireworks for general retail sale (UN category

---

[5] Explosives Regulations 2014 SI 2014:1638

1.4G). However, a small number of category 3 fireworks contain more than 25g of flash powder and, therefore, come under a category of explosives with a 'minor blast hazard' (UN category 1.3G) and require additional storage requirements.

The licence permits the sale of fireworks as follows unless the licence holder applies for an 'All Year Road Licence':

- The three days leading up to and on the first day of the Chinese New Year
- The three days leading up to and on Diwali
- During the period 15th October to 10th November
- During the period 26th December to 31st December

The local licensing authority has the power to revoke or refuse the licence if the holder has committed certain offences, including under age sales offences. Appeal lies to the Magistrates' Court.

7.10    Enforcement

By virtue of Regulation 18 (1), it is the duty of the local weights and measures authority (Trading Standards Department) to enforce the provisions of the Pyrotechnic Articles (Safety) Regulations 2010 within their area.

In addition, the Secretary of State for Business, Innovation and Skills may enforce the regulations, but this would be unlikely for age restricted sales offences.

Trading Standards are required to carry out regular inspections of fireworks at storage sites, with the Health and Safety Executive having responsibility to inspect manufacturing sites.

Section 27 (1) of the Consumer Protection Act 1987 places a duty on the local weights and measures authority (Trading Standards Department) to enforce safety provisions within their area. This includes the provisions under the Fireworks Regulation 2004 and Pyrotechnic Articles (Safety) Regulations 2010.

Unlike most underage sales legislation, enforcement officers have extensive powers of investigation for breaches of these Regulations. In particular, powers to enter and inspect premises, seize and detain documents, seize and detain goods and records and undertake test purchases. For more on officer's powers see section 11.1 *post*.

7.11    Penalties

The penalties for offences are expressed as maximum levels based upon the standard scale[6] applicable in Magistrates' Courts. All of the offences set out in this section are 'summary only' and may only be tried in the Magistrates' Courts.

EA1875 – Explosives Act 1875
PTAR2010 – Pyrotechnic Articles (Safety) Regulations 2010

Level One - £200 maximum

Level Two - £500 maximum

Level Three - £1,000 maximum

Level Four - £2,500 maximum

Level Five - unlimited fine

S.31 – EA1875 – Supply of gunpowder to children
R.15(2) – PTAR2010 – Supply of a category 2 or category 3 firework to a person under 18 years
R.15(1)(a) – PTAR2010 – Supply of a Christmas cracker to a person under 12 years
R.15(1)(b) – PTAR2010 – Supply of a category 1 firework to a person under 16 years
R.33(2) – PTAR2010 – Supply of a category T1 or category P1 pyrotechnic article to a person under 18 years (note: and/or up to three months imprisonment – and potential for trial on indictment or referral to the Crown Court for an unlimited fine and/or up to two years imprisonment)[7]

---

[6] S.37(2), Criminal Justice Act 1982 as amended by s.85 of the Legal Aid, Sentencing and Punishment of Offenders Act 2012
[7] By virtue of Regulation 39

CHAPTER EIGHT

# VIDEOS, DVDS, GAMES AND HARMFUL PUBLICATIONS

## CONTENTS

8.1    Introduction

The 2010 collation agreement between the Conservatives and Liberal Democrats included a commitment to:

'Take action to protect children from excessive commercialisation and premature sexualisation.'

Reg Bailey, Chairman of the Mothers' Union was commissioned to undertake a review of the commercialisation and sexualisation of childhood. In his report[1], he focusses on the 'wallpaper of children's lives' and highlights the growing sexualised culture:

> 'We are all living in an increasingly sexual and sexualised culture, although it is far from clear how we arrived at this point. Many parents feel that this culture is often inappropriate for their children... sexualised and gender-stereotyped clothing, products and services for children are the biggest areas of concern.'

In his review, he called for greater regulation of adult content, including introducing age ratings for music videos, restrictions on adult online content, a retail code of good practice on retailing to children and stricter controls on advertising.

This section sets out the existing controls on exposure of children to sexual, violent or inappropriate imagery.

8.2    Key Legislation

Children and Young Persons (Harmful Publications) Act 1955
Licensing Act 2003
Local Government (Miscellaneous Provisions) Act 1982
Video Recordings Act 1984[2]

---

[1] *Letting Children be Children: Report of an Independent Review of the Commercialisation and Sexualisation of Childhood* (2011) HM Government Cm 8078

[2] Due to a technical error when this Act was originally passed, it was necessary to repeal and re-enact the legislation by the Video Recordings Act 2010. This had no practical effect on the provisions other than the suspension of enforcement during the transition period.

8.3    Summary of Age Restricted Laws relating to Videos, DVDs, Games and Harmful Publications

- It is illegal to supply a classified video work to a person who has not attained the age of classification, unless it is an exempted supply
- It is a defence to show either that the seller did not know the age of classification, reasonably believed the purchaser to be over the age of classification or reasonably believed it to be an exempted supply
- It is a defence to show that the seller took all reasonable precautions and exercised all due diligence to avoid the commission of the offence
- A person may be imprisoned for up to six months or an unlimited fine, or both, for a breach
- A supply is exempted if it is not for reward and not in the course of a business
- There are a number of other, quite complex, exempted supplies that apply in specific circumstances
- It is a breach of licensing conditions (and therefore an offence) to operate a cinema premises in such a manner as to breach the age classifications on films
- A person may be imprisoned for up to six months or an unlimited fine or both for a breach
- It is illegal to sell or let for hire harmful publications to a person under the age of 18 years
- It is illegal to print, publish or import harmful publications. A harmful publication is any book, magazine or other like work which is likely to fall into the hands of children and contains picture portraying the commission of crime, acts of violence and cruelty, or incidents of a repulsive or horrible nature in such a way that it is likely to corrupt a child or young person
- The above offences carry a £1,000 fine, up to 51 weeks in prison, or both, in a Magistrates Court
- It is a defence to show that the offender had not examined the material and had no reasonable cause to suspect that it was a harmful publication

8.4    Classified Video Works and Films

Most videos, DVDs, Blu Ray discs and films for cinema exhibition are classified depending upon their content. In addition, some video games are classified. The classification is undertaken by the British Board of Film Classification[3] and enforcement is undertaken by local trading standards authorities.

The classifications are:

**U - Universal**. It is impossible to predict what might upset any particular child. But a 'U' film should be suitable for all audiences. 'U' films should be set within a positive moral framework and should offer reassuring counterbalances to any violence, threat or horror.

If a work is particularly suitable for a pre-school child to view alone, this will be indicated by the consumer advice. Previously, the BBFC issued a 'Uc' certificate, indicating a video work that was particularly suitable for children. This has now been withdrawn, but previously classified 'Uc' films remain in circulation.

**PG Parental Guidance**. General viewing, but some scenes may be unsuitable for young children. Unaccompanied children of any age may watch and a 'PG' film should not disturb a child aged around 8 or older. However, parents are advised to consider whether the content may upset younger or more sensitive children.

**12 & 12A rated films**. Exactly the same criteria are used to classify works at '12A' and '12'. These categories are awarded where the material is suitable, in general, only for those aged 12 and over. Works classified at these categories may upset children under 12 or contain material which many parents will find unsuitable for them.

The '12A' category exists only for cinema films. No one younger than 12 may see a '12A' film in a cinema unless accompanied by an adult, and films classified '12A' are not recommended for a child below 12. An adult may take a younger child if, in their judgement, the film is suitable for that particular child. In such circumstances, responsibility for allowing a child under 12 to view lies with the accompanying adult.

The '12' category exists only for video works. No one younger than 12 may rent or buy a '12' rated video work.

**15 rated films**. No one younger than 15 may see a '15' film in a cinema. No one younger than 15 may rent or buy a '15' rated video work

**18 & R18 rated films**. No one younger than 18 may see an '18' film in a cinema. No one younger than 18 may rent or buy an '18' rated video work.

The 'R18' category is a special and legally restricted classification primarily for explicit works of consenting sex or strong fetish material involving adults. Films may only be shown to adults in specially licensed cinemas, and video works may be supplied to adults only in licensed sex shops (see section 8.8, *post*). 'R18' videos may not be supplied by mail order.

The video classification is required to be shown on the video work and the sleeve or cover of the video work[3].

Section 11 (1) of the Video Recordings Act 1984 prohibits the supply of a classified video work to a person who has not attained that age.

It is a defence to show that the supplier did not know, or had no reason to believe, that the classification certificate contained the age restriction.

It is a defence to show that the supplier did not know, or had no reason to believe, that the purchaser had not attained the relevant age.

There are exemptions that apply relating to various circumstances including educational works, trade-to-trade supplies and for international transactions (outside the UK).

Occasionally, classified DVDs are being distributed attached to magazines or newspapers, however, with the advent of download and streaming services this practice is declining. This will mean that retailers will need to be vigilant for any such DVDs, which tend to be in supplements or attached to video games magazines. The Department of Culture, Media and Sport have advised Trading Standards Officers that they do not believe the magazine or newspaper as a 'cover' for the DVD requires to be labelled with the video classification in addition to the DVD or its sleeve. However, if the newspaper, magazine or its packaging obscure the DVD cover, then the video classification would have to appear on the outer packaging. It is common for games magazines containing DVDs to be wrapped in plastic or foil opaque packaging and, in such cases, the video classification is required to be shown on the outer packaging[4].

By S.20 of the Licensing Act 2003, any premises licensed for the exhibition of films must have a mandatory condition on the licence concerning adherence with either the classification of films by the BBFC or the local licensing authority. Local authorities only have powers to overrule the BBFC classification in relation to cinema screenings, not in relation to rental or sale videos or DVDs.

Local authorities generally accept the BBFC's recommendation for a certificate for a film. There have been some notable exceptions – particularly in the 1970s

---

[3] Video Recordings (Labelling) Regulations 1985
[4] R.4(5) Video Recordings (Labelling) Regulations 1985

when the BBFC allowed films such as *Last Tango in Paris* and *The Exorcist* to be released with an 'X' certificate (essentially the same as today's '18') – but many local authorities chose to ban the films regardless.

Conversely, in 2002, a few local authorities, apparently under pressure from distributors and cinema chains, ignored the BBFC's ruling that *Spider-Man* receive a '12' rating, and allowed children younger than 12 to see the film. However, the BBFC were already in the process of replacing the '12' rating with a new '12A', which allowed under 12s to see the film if accompanied by an adult, so shortly afterwards, *Spider-Man* was reclassified as '12A'.

The failure to comply with a film classification in a cinema is not a direct offence, but would be a breach of a licence condition under S.136 (1) of the Licensing Act 2003. It should be noted that this carries a substantial penalty of an unlimited fine and/or up to six months in prison, or to both. In addition, the licence of the cinema can be reviewed (see section 2.7, *ante*)

8.5      On-Demand Programme Services

From 1st December 2014, it is a breach of Part 4A of the Communications Act 2003 for an on-demand programme service to contain any specially restricted material unless the material is made available in a manner which secures that persons under the age of 18 will not normally see or hear it[5].

"Specially restricted material" means:

(a) A video work in respect of which the BBFC has issued a R18 classification certificate,
(b) material whose nature is such that it is reasonable to expect that, if the material were contained in a video work submitted to the video works authority for a classification certificate, the video works authority would issue a R18 classification certificate, or
(c) other material that might seriously impair the physical, mental or moral development of persons under the age of 18.

These provisions are enforced by the Authority for Television on Demand (ATVOD)[6] on behalf of the Office for Communications (OFCOM)

---

[7] S.368E(1) Communications Act 2003 as inserted by R.2 of the Audiovisual Media Services Regulations 2014 (SI:2014:2916)
[6] http://www.atvod.co.uk/

A service is an on-demand programme service if its principal purpose is the provision of television of film programmes on-demand, there is a person who has editorial responsibility for it in the jurisdiction of the United Kingdom and it is made available for use by members of the public.

OFCOM are empowered to impose large financial penalties for breach of these provisions including a fine of up to 5% of the provider's revenue or £250,000 whichever is the greater.

ATVOD have set out detailed guidance on the matters that it will consider in its approach to determining breaches of these provisions. ATVOD's approach in the first instance is to determine whether the content in question falls within the definition of 'specially restricted material'. Content whose broadcast complies with the Ofcom Broadcasting Code, or that has been classified by the British Board of Film Classification (BBFC) in any category except 'R18' or 'R18-equivalent material', would not normally be considered material that "might seriously impair" and would not normally be considered as specially restricted material.  These restrictions would not therefore apply to normal '18, '15' or '12' age restricted video works.

All 'material' on the service, including still images and other non-video content is subject to these requirements. There is no requirement for material being provided on an on demand programme service to be classified by the BBFC, but ATVOD is required to have regard to the BBFC Classification Guidelines when determining whether material is R18-equivalent.

Provided the material is not illegal or otherwise prohibited, content which ATVOD considers to fall under this Rule (i.e. 'specially restricted material') may be made available in an on demand programme service provided access is controlled in a manner which secures that persons under eighteen 'will not normally see or hear' such material. ATVOD's interpretation of this requirement is that there should be in place an effective Content Access Control System ("CAC System") which verifies that the user is aged 18 or over at the point of registration or access by the mandatory use of technical tools for age verification and, if age verification does not take place each time the user returns to the service, controls further access to such content when the user returns to the service by the use of mandatory security controls such as passwords or PIN numbers.

Technical tools which may be acceptable for age verification purposes include:

- Confirmation of credit card ownership or other form of payment where mandatory proof that the holder is 18 or over is required prior to issue[7].

- A reputable personal digital identity management service which uses checks on an independent and reliable database, such as the electoral roll.
- Other comparable proof of account ownership which effectively verifies age. For example, possession and ownership of an effectively age-verified mobile phone[8].

Where they are required, CAC Systems must be fit for purpose and effectively managed so as to ensure that in ATVOD's opinion persons under the age of eighteen will not normally see or hear specially restricted material. ATVOD will consider the adequacy and effectiveness of CAC Systems on a case by case basis and keep them under review in the context of on-demand programme services. Responsibility for ensuring that any required CAC System is in place and is operating effectively rests at all times with the person with editorial responsibility for the on demand programme service.

On 27th April 2015, ATVOD set out its final determination[9] in the matter of "GLASGOW MISTRESS MEGARA FURIE" a service that ATVOD described as 'adult fetish material'. In this case, ATVOD visited their website and was prompted to confirm that:

> "You are 18 years of age or older (21- years old where 18 is not the age of majority) and that you are voluntarily choosing to view and access such sexually-explicit images and content for your own personal use..."

ATVOD could click through and view certain still images and sample video works of adult fetish material without any further age verification. In addition, ATVOD was able to pay-per-view further adult material by paying with a debit card, a pre-paid card or a bank funds transfer from banks in any of 10 EU countries. In all cases, no further age verification checks were in place. ATVOD determined that the service provider had, therefore, failed to

---

[7] ATVOD will not regard confirmation of ownership of a Debit, Solo or Electron card or any other card where the card holder is not required to be 18 or over to be verification that a user of a service is aged 18 or over.

[8] 'Mobile phone' here refers to the SIM card rather than the physical handset. For a phone to be effectively age-verified the account holder must have presented proof of identity and age (for example driving licence or valid passport) to the mobile phone operator. An effective CAC system must establish that the owner of the effectively age-verified phone is the person attempting to access content – for example by demonstrating possession of the phone and awareness of the attempted access. As with other age verification methods, mandatory security controls such as passwords or PIN numbers may be used for subsequent access to the service.

[9] http://www.atvod.co.uk/uploads/files/Rule_11_FD_Megara_Furie_FOR_PUBLICATION.pdf

ensure that the adult material would not be available to persons under the age of eighteen.

8.6     Pan-European Games Information (PEGI)

From 30th July 2012, the classification of video games became statutory by virtue of the Video Recordings (Labelling) Regulations 2012[10].

The Pan-European Games Information (PEGI) classification is administered by the Games Rating Agency (a subsidiary of the Video Standards Council).

The PEGI labels appear on front and back of the packaging indicating one of the following age levels: 3, 7, 12, 16 and 18. They provide a reliable indication of the suitability of the game content in terms of protection of minors. The age rating does not take into account the difficulty level or skills required to play a game. Only those games marked 12, 16 or 18 are legally enforceable, the other ratings are for guidance only.

PEGI 3
The content of games given this rating is considered suitable for all age groups. Some violence in a comical context (typically *Bugs Bunny* or *Tom & Jerry* cartoon-like forms of violence) is acceptable. The child should not be able to associate the character on the screen with real life characters, they should be totally fantasy. The game should not contain any sounds or pictures that are likely to scare or frighten young children. No bad language should be heard.

PEGI 7
Any game that would normally be rated at 3 but contains some possibly frightening scenes or sounds may be considered suitable in this category.

PEGI 12
Video games that show violence of a slightly more graphic nature towards fantasy character and/or non-graphic violence towards human-looking characters or recognisable animals, as well as video games that show nudity of a slightly more graphic nature, would fall in this age category. Any bad language in this category must be mild and fall short of sexual expletives.

PEGI 16
This rating is applied once the depiction of violence (or sexual activity) reaches

---

[10] Video Recordings (Labelling) Regulations 2012 (SI2012:1767)

a stage that looks the same as would be expected in real life. More extreme bad language, the concept of the use of tobacco and drugs and the depiction of criminal activities can be content of games that are rated 16.

PEGI 18
The adult classification is applied when the level of violence reaches a stage where it becomes a depiction of gross violence and/or includes elements of specific types of violence. Gross violence is the most difficult to define since it can be very subjective in many cases, but in general terms it can be classed as the depictions of violence that would make the viewer feel a sense of revulsion.

Descriptors shown on the back of the packaging indicate the main reasons why a game has received a particular age rating. There are eight such descriptors: violence, bad language, fear, drugs, sexual, discrimination, gambling and online gameplay with other people.

8.7     Harmful Publications

A 'harmful publication' is any book, magazine or other like work which is of a kind likely to fall into the hands of children or young persons. It consists wholly or mainly of stories told in pictures (with or without the addition of written matter) being stories portraying –

- The commission of crimes
- Acts of violence or cruelty
- Incidents of a repulsive or horrible nature

in such a way that the work as a whole would tend to corrupt the child or young person into whose hands it might fall.
The Children and Young Persons (Harmful Publications) Act 1955 was introduced to address concerns about comics, mainly from the USA, that were around at the time. The legislation is very rarely used and there have been no attempts to enforce it since the 1960s.

The Act does not create a direct 'age restriction' in the sense that age restrictions for alcohol, cigarettes or other restricted goods are provided in legislation. In fact, it is only implied that an offence would be made out if a seller of such publications sold them directly to a person under the age of 18 years. However, the offence would also be made out if it could be shown that the publication was supplied to a person over the age of 18 years, but was likely to fall into the hands of children or young people.

The legislation was aimed specifically at certain 1950s comics, mainly from America, and followed a long public campaign to get them banned. The objectionable comics included *Batman*, *Whiz Comics*, *Creatures*, *Mad Monsters* and *Horror Monsters*. The government of the day eventually relented and published proposals to ban the comics in 1954[11], leading to the 1955 Act.

In an attempt to address the concerns, the US Comic Code Authority was created and established a code of practice for the contents and marketing of comics, the breach of which could form a *prima facie* case that the publication could be harmful. The code includes provision that:

- Crimes shall never be presented in such a way as to create sympathy for the criminal, to promote distrust of the forces of law and justice, or to inspire others with a desire to imitate criminals
- If crime is depicted, it shall be as a sordid and unpleasant activity
- Criminals shall not be presented so as to be rendered glamorous, or to occupy a position which creates a desire for emulation
- In every instance good shall triumph over evil and the criminal punished for his misdeeds
- Scenes of excessive violence shall be prohibited. Scenes of brutal torture, excessive and unnecessary knife and gunplay, physical agony, gory and gruesome crime shall be eliminated
- No comic magazine shall use the word horror or terror in its title
- All scenes of horror, excessive bloodshed, gory or gruesome crimes, depravity, lust, sadism, masochism shall not be permitted
- All lurid, unsavoury, gruesome illustrations shall be eliminated
- Inclusion of stories dealing with evil shall be used or shall be published only where the intent is to illustrate a moral issue, and in no case shall evil be presented alluringly, nor so as to injure the sensibilities of the reader
- Scenes dealing with, or instruments associated with, walking dead, torture, vampires and vampirism, ghouls, cannibalism, and werewolfism are prohibited
- Profanity, obscenity, smut, vulgarity, or words or symbols which have acquired undesirable meanings are forbidden
- Nudity in any form is prohibited, as is indecent or undue exposure
- Suggestive and salacious illustration or suggestive posture is unacceptable
- Females shall be drawn realistically, without exaggeration of any physical qualities
- Illicit sex relations are neither to be hinted at nor portrayed. Violent love scenes, as well as sexual abnormalities, are unacceptable
- Seduction and rape shall never be shown or suggested

---

[11] Prime Ministers' Office (PREM 11/858) 1954 – proposed legislation to tackle harmful comics

- Sex perversion or any inference to same is strictly forbidden
- Nudity with meretricious purpose and salacious postures shall not be permitted in the advertising of any product; clothed figures shall never be presented in such a way as to be offensive or contrary to good taste or morals

Whether or not a publication can be considered harmful is a highly subjective question of fact for the Magistrates to determine. A child is defined as being under 14 years of age and young person is defined as being between 14 and 18 years of age[12]. However, the remainder of the section is undefined and there is no direct case law.

The legislation requires the consent of the Attorney General[13] before proceedings can be instituted in England and Wales. The Solicitor General has delegated authority in certain circumstances to make the decision on behalf of the Attorney General[14].

There have only been eight applications made for prosecutions, the last one being in 1965. All eight applications were declined by the Attorney General. The legislation was initially passed with a 'sunset clause' and was due to expire after 10 years on 31st December 1965. However, this was repealed by the Expiring Laws Act 1969, S.1 and so the Act remains in force, but it appears has not been actively pursued since 1965.

As this is 1950s legislation, there is no reference to any information technology, but the definition of any 'relevant work' prohibited by the Act does include 'photographic film' as an alternative media, so it is likely that publication would be held to include publication over the Internet.

It is irrelevant where the internet publication emanates from, i.e. in which country the server is located, provided the relevant publication has been downloaded within the UK[15].

## 8.8    Human Rights

It has been suggested by campaigners against censorship that the legislation controlling entertainment is an unlawful interference with the right to freedom

---

[12] See S.5(2) Children and Young Persons (Harmful Publications) Act 1955 and s.107 Children and Young Persons Act 1933

[13] See S.2(2) Children and Young Persons (Harmful Publications) Act 1955

[14] See S.1 Law Officers Act 1944

[15] *R v Perrin* [2002] EWCA 747

of expression[16]. This right, enshrined in UK law by the Human Rights Act 1998, derives from Article 10 of the European Convention on Human Rights.

Article 10 includes:

> 'Freedom to hold opinions and to receive and impart information and ideas without interference by public authority and regardless of frontiers.'

Article 10(2) goes on to say that:

> 'The exercise of these freedoms, since it carries with it duties and responsibilities, may be subject to such formalities, conditions, restrictions or penalties as are prescribed by law and are necessary in a democratic society in the interests of...public safety, for the prevention of disorder or crime, for the protection of health or morals, protection of the reputation or rights of other...'

Any restriction on freedom of expression that is imposed by national law must be capable of objective justification as being necessary in a democratic society, for one of the purposes set out. The so called 'margin of appreciation' enables states to have a degree of latitude to decide law and social policy in the light of their own cultures and values. It is likely that this Act would be covered by that 'margin of appreciation', but it has never been tested in the courts.

In *R (Handyside) v United Kingdom*[17], the European Court of Human Rights had to consider the legality of the Obscenity Acts 1959 and 1964:

> 'Sharing the view of the Government and the unanimous opinion of the Commission, the court finds that the Obscenity Acts 1959 and 1964 have an aim that is legitimate under Article 10(2), namely, the protection of morals in a democratic society' (para 46).

The majority of the Commission agreed that the European Court had only to ensure that the United Kingdom courts acted reasonably, in good faith and within the limits of the margin of appreciation left to Contracting States by Article 10(2):

---

[16] See particularly *Wingrove v United Kingdom* (1997) 24 EHRR 1 as a case involving refusal by BBFC to classify a video work that it considered would cause offence and shock.
[17] [1976] ECHR 5

*'There was no uniform conception of morals. State authorities were better placed than the international judge to assess the necessity for a restriction designed to protect morals'* (para.2)

In the expression 'necessary in a democratic society' (Article 10(2)), the word 'necessary' was not synonymous with 'indispensable', but implied the existence of a pressing social need (para.2).

By S.2 (1) of the Act, there is a defence of innocent publication, dissemination, sale or letting for hire.

This Act pre-dates the evolution of the reasonable precautions and due diligence defence in statutory strict liability offences. However, any actions taken to avoid commission of the offences would still amount to mitigation if any proceedings were instituted, and would be a matter that the Attorney General would take into account before authorising any prosecution under the Act.

Although there have never been any recorded prosecutions under this Act, anyone engaged in the organised importation or distribution of harmful publications is likely to face imprisonment. In *R v Hirst*[18] the Court of Appeal upheld a sentence of 12 months' imprisonment on a plea of guilty by a 51 year-old with no convictions to conspiracy to import obscene videos in a 'sophisticated operation' in which the offender had an 'important role'.

## 8.9     Adult Magazines

There is no specific legislation providing age restrictions for adult magazines, pornographic magazines, 'lads' or 'ladies' magazines or explicit newspapers.

However, in partnership with publishers of these titles, the National Federation of Retail Newsagents has published a code of practice which includes provision for:

### 8.9.1    Adult Top-Shelf Titles

- That adult titles should be displayed on the top shelf only and out of the reach of children
- That adult titles should not be sold to any person under the age of 18 years
- That adult titles should only be acquired from bona fide trade channels (on

---

[18] [2001] 1 Cr App R (S) 44

the basis that these will have been vetted by the suppliers' lawyers for compliance with legislation)
- That care and sensitivity be exercised over the display of adult titles with explicit front covers

8.9.2    'Lads mags' (and 'ladies mags') with front covers or content that may offend some customers

- That they should not be displayed at children's eye-level or below, to ensure that they are not in the direct sight and reach of children
- That they should not be displayed adjacent to the display of children's titles and comics
- Where display space restraints preclude the above, titles with front covers that may cause concern are part-overlapped with other titles so as to minimise the potential for offence to parents with children

8.9.3    Other Titles and National Newspapers

- Newspapers can be folded in half so that the masthead and price is exposed, but the front cover picture is not
- On a plinth display, newspapers can be overlapped with other newspapers to leave the masthead and price exposed, but not the front page picture
- Where a title carries a masthead on the back page, as well as the front, display the back page uppermost

8.10    Sex Shops, Sex Cinemas, Lap Dancing Clubs and Materials for Sexual Activity

There are four types of legal sex establishment:

- An unlicensed shop or online establishment that supplies materials for sexual activity (but not R18 classified video works)
- A licensed sex shop that supplies materials for sexual activity including R18 classified video works
- A licensed sex cinema that displays R18 classified video works (but may not supply materials for sexual activity)
- A licensed sexual entertainment centre commonly referred to as a lap dancing club.

Other premises offering sexual services in return for payment are likely to be unlawful[19].

---

[19] S.33A, Sexual Offences Act 1956

Any item used for the purposes of birth control during sexual activity (such as condoms) are exempt from controls. There are no age restrictions for such items in any premises, although it would be an offence for a person aged under 16 to use them for sexual activity[20].

There are no specific age restrictions in place for goods supplied from an unlicensed sex shop. This includes online sex shops, which do not require licensing. It should be noted that unlicensed sex shops are not permitted to supply R18 classified video works.

There are a number of online sex shops and some well-known high street names with stores that supply materials for sexual activity. Other than general restrictions described elsewhere in this book, there are no specific age restrictions at these stores.

Licenses for sex establishments are issued by local licensing authorities. The conditions applicable to those licences vary considerably; however, by Paragraph 23 of Schedule 3 to the Local Government (Miscellaneous Provisions) Act 1982, no holder of a sex establishment licence may:

- Without reasonable excuse knowingly permit a person under the age of 18 years to enter the premises or
- Employ a person known to him to be under the age of 18 years in the business of the establishment

Local licensing conditions can also add requirements for:

- Signage warning of age restrictions
- Evidence requirements for proof of age (these can be particularly strict for people working in sex entertainment centres)
- Additional precautions necessary to prevent under age admission

Licensed sex shops are permitted to have online sites (which are in effect unlicensed supplies), but they are not permitted to distribute R18 classified videos otherwise than within the confines of the licensed sex shop[21].

---

[20] Most local NHS Services support the 'C Card' – a card available to young people aged 14 – 24 giving them access to free condoms subject to them attending a guidance session on sexual safety. This card is not available to those aged 13 or under, but they can still purchase condoms from retailers.
[21] *Interfact Limited and Anor v Liverpool City Council* [2005] EWHC 995 (Admin)

Often normal cinemas have a licence as a sex cinema so that they can occasionally show R18 films to patrons. In such circumstances, when operating as a sex cinema (or having a screen operating as a sex cinema) they will normally be required to post a notice outside stating:

> 'Persons under 18 cannot be admitted to this cinema/screen for any part of the programme.'

There may also be requirements on the licence as to door supervision and segregation of patrons.

Some local licensing authorities prohibit sex cinemas operating at the same time as non-sex cinemas in a multi-screen complex, or require advance consent for this. Where this is the case, they will normally be required to post a notice at each entrance stating:

> 'Cinema Club – Members and Guests Only. Persons under 18 cannot be admitted to this cinema for any part of the programme.'

Where a cinema club is in place, licence conditions usually require membership of both sexes and all members to have to prove that they are over 18 years of age. Usually, the sale or marketing of materials used for sexual activity is prohibited in sex cinemas.

Licenses for sexual entertainment venues will normally require the licence holder to take steps to ensure that all performers are over 18. Typically, there is a requirement to see photographic identification and to keep a copy of this on file for inspection. Usually, the sale or marketing of materials used for sexual activity is prohibited in sex entertainment venues.

## 8.11   Enforcement

There are no specific duties of enforcement for controls on harmful publications, but the powers of enforcement contained in S.3 relate to a police constable. They include powers of search under warrant and seizure of offending articles.

It is the duty of the local licensing authority to enforce the controls at licensed sex establishments. Together with the police, they have extensive powers of entry and inspection of records.

8.12    Penalties

The penalties for offences are expressed as maximum levels based upon the standard scale[22] applicable in Magistrates' Courts. All of the offences set out in this section are 'summary only' and may only be tried in the Magistrates' Courts.

HPA1955 – Children and Young Persons (Harmful Publications) Act 1955
LGMPA1982 – Local Government (Miscellaneous Provisions) Act 1982
VRA1984 – Video Recordings Act 1984

Level One - £200 maximum

Level Two - £500 maximum

Level Three - £1,000 maximum

S.2(1) – HPA1955 – Sell, let or hire harmful publications (note: and/or imprisonment for a term not exceeding four months[23])

Level Four - £2,500 maximum

Level Five - unlimited fine

S.11(1) – VRA1984 – Supply of a video work in contravention of the age classification (note: and/or imprisonment for up to six months)

General

Unlimited fine - S.136 (1) – LA2003 – Operating otherwise than in accordance with an authorisation (licence), such as failing to comply with mandatory conditions concerning film classifications (note: This offence also carries a potential prison sentence of up to six months in addition to or instead of a fine)
Unlimited fine – P.23, Sch 3 – LGMPA1982 – Permitting or employing a person under 18 in a licensed sex establishment (note: this offence also carries a potential prison sentence of up to six months in addition to or instead of a fine)

---

[22] S.37(2), Criminal Justice Act 1982 as amended by s.85 of the Legal Aid, Sentencing and Punishment of Offenders Act 2012
[23] Provision has been made in Schedule 26, Paragraph 15 of the Criminal Justice Act 2003 to raise the penalty for imprisonment from four months to 51 weeks, but no day has yet been appointed to bring that provision into force.

CHAPTER NINE

# OTHER AGE RESTRICTED GOODS AND SERVICES

## CONTENTS

CONTENTS

9.1      Introduction

There are a broad range of other products and services that are age restricted, some by the creation of criminal offences, some as a result of civil contractual matters. This chapter sets out the remaining key legislation relating to these other goods.

9.2      Key Legislation

Tattooing of Minors Act 1969
Female Genital Mutilation Act 2003
Hypnotism Act 1952
Sunbeds (Regulation) Act 2010
Animal Welfare Act 2006
Consumer Credit Act 1974
Sale of Goods Act 1979

9.3      Summary of Age Restricted Laws relating to Other Products

- It is an offence to tattoo a person under 18 years (except for medical reasons)
- It is an offence to pierce the genitalia of a person under 16 years, which for girls includes nipples, aurora and breasts (except for medical reasons)
- It is an offence to give an exhibition, demonstration or performance of hypnotism at or in connection with public entertainment on a person under the age of 18 years
- It is an offence for a person involved in carrying on a sunbed business to allow or permit a person under 18 years to use a sunbed or to be in a restricted zone
- It is an offence to sell, transfer or gift an animal to a person under the age of 16 years
- It is an offence to enter into an arrangement with a person under the age of 16 years where a prize may be an animal
- It is an offence for a person, with a view to financial gain, to send to a person under the age 18 years any document inviting him to borrow money, obtain goods or services on credit or apply for information or advice about borrowing money

- Although not an offence, a contract with a person under the age of 18 is unenforceable against that person unless the goods or services were necessaries for the basic needs of living (such as food, shelter, clothing, etc)
- There are proposals to introduce a requirement for information society providers (like social networking sites) to gain positive parental consent for users under 13 years of age.
- It is an offence to offer financial inducements to a person under 16 years of age to participate in a clinical trial
- It is an offence to administer strong teeth whitening products to any person under 18 years of age

## 9.4   Tattoos

The Royal Navy now actively discourages tattooing, but there was a time when it was both commonplace and expected of young ratings to get tattoos. In the 1960s, children were regularly getting tattoos and the defence of tattoo artists was that the children had given their consent in a free society.

This changed with the case of *Burrell v Harmer* [1]. In that case, a tattooist was charged with assault occasioning actual bodily harm on two boys aged 12 and 13. He claimed a defence of consent. The court held that, whilst consent was a valid defence, where the victim was unable to appreciate the nature of the act he was ostensibly consenting to, that was no real consent at all. Although reference was made to the two boys being minors, the court did not create a clear cut 'age of consent' for tattooing, merely a question of fact as to whether or not the child was capable of understanding the consequences of their consent.

In 1969, the Tattooing of Minors Act was introduced following the introduction of a Private Members Bill by Martin Madden, MP. By section 1 of this Act it is illegal to tattoo a person under the age of 18 years.

It is a defence to show that the tattooist reasonably believed the person to be over 18.

A tattoo performed by a medical practitioner for a medical purpose is exempt. It is common for young people that have had an appendix removed for the surgeon to mark that it has been removed by a tattoo.

The penalty for breaches is now set as a fine of up to £1,000 for each breach.

---

[1] [1969] Crim LR 169D

The tattoo must be inserted into the skin and be a permanent mark. 'Henna' tattoos are, therefore, not covered by the legislation.

9.5      Body Piercing

There is no specific offence relating to body piercing of minors. Body piercing is covered by an industry code of practice, which stipulates that piercings should not be undertaken on anyone under the age of 14 years. However, often this is ignored for ear piercing. The code of practice also states that any person aged 14 years to 16 years should bring a parent or guardian with them. It suggests that 'below the neck' piercings are at the discretion of the piercer aged 14 years to 16 years. Any person over 16 years of age is considered to be an adult for the purposes of this code. The code of practice is managed by the British Body Piercing Association and is available at http://www.bbpa.org.uk/ethics.html.

However, care needs to be taken regarding the issue of whether a child is capable of giving consent to body piercing.

In theory, a child can only give consent to an assault occasioning actual bodily harm if they are capable of understanding the nature of the harm and the consequences of it[2]. There are some matters of public policy during which consent cannot be given. For instance, a child cannot consent to an assault of a sexual nature (which includes piercing of their breasts, penis, vagina or anus). It is also highly questionable whether a parent can give consent to any kind of piercing on the child's behalf. Although the law does provide certain conditions (known as 'Gillick' competence[3]) where a parent can give consent to an assault on their child, these are invariably associated with treatment for medical conditions and would be unlikely to apply to piercing for cosmetic purposes.

Nevertheless, piercing of children, particularly ear piercing is commonplace. There is no direct prohibition for it and most ear piercing shops follow a simple consent process, involving the agreement of parents or guardians for those under the age of 16 years. Most will not pierce cartilage.

9.5.1 Genitalia

Very particular care needs to be taken with piercing breasts, vagina or anal areas of girls, or penis or anal areas of boys. It would be likely to be considered as a

---

[2] Burrell v Harmer [1969] Crim LR 169D
[3] Gillick v West Norfolk Area Health Authority [1986] 1 AC 112;

sexual assault on anyone under the age of 16 years. This can result in a penalty of up to 14 years imprisonment and inclusion on the sex offenders' register.

In addition, by section 1 of the Female Genital Mutilation Act 2003, it is an offence to excise, infibulate or otherwise mutilate the whole or any part of a girl's labia majora, labia minora or clitoris. This is defined by the United Nations and World Health Organisation as including piercing of genitalia[4]. Although female genital mutilation is usually carried out for ritual or custom reasons on girls under the age of 15 years, it should be noted that this legislation applies to older women as well, so this is not strictly age restricted legislation. The penalty for this offence is up to 14 years imprisonment and/or an unlimited fine.

## 9.6    Hypnotism

By section 3 of the Hypnotism Act 1952, it is an offence for a person to give an exhibition, demonstration or performance of hypnotism on a person who has not attained the age of 18 years[5]. It should be noted that it has to be at or in connection with an entertainment to which the public are admitted, whether on payment or otherwise.

It is a defence for the hypnotist to show that he had reasonable cause to believe that the person was over 18.

The penalty for an offence is a fine of up to £1,000. The powers for a police officer to enter premises without warrant relating to this Act were abolished by the Protection of Freedoms Act 2012.

The legislation does not apply to any hypnotism for scientific or research purposes, or for the treatment of mental or physical disease.

## 9.7    Sunbeds

Sunbeds are one of the newest products to be age restricted following a long campaign to clamp down on tanning shops. The legislation was introduced by a Private Members Bill and became the Sunbeds (Regulation) Act 2010. It came into force on 8th April 2011.

---

[4] World Health Organisation, Factsheet 241, Female Genital Mutilation, February 2012
[5] This was reduced from 21 years by the Family Law Reform Act 1969, s.1(3), Sch.1 Para 1

It is an offence for a sunbed business to allow or invite a person under 18 years of age to use a sunbed. It is also an offence to allow a person under 18 years of age to be in a restricted zone, which includes a room or partition containing a sunbed. This means that sunbed users aged over 18 are not permitted to take their children into a restricted zone, even if their children are not using the sunbed. There is no lower limit on this restriction, so a baby in a pram would not be permitted in a restricted zone.

It is a defence to show that the offender took all reasonable precautions and exercised all due diligence to avoid the offence. The penalty for a breach is an unlimited fine.

The legislation does not apply to sunbeds in a hospital where the sunbed is used under the direction of a registered medical practitioner.

9.7.1 Sunbed Legislation in WALES only

There are additional provisions that apply in Wales only at the moment, but may in due course be extended to England.

It is an offence for a sunbed business to allow or invite a person under 18 years of age to use a sunbed in domestic premises. It is an offence to sell or hire a sunbed to a person under 18 years of age.

The penalty for a breach of these provisions is an unlimited fine.

9.8      Pet Animals

The legislation on the welfare of pets and animals was consolidated into the Animal Welfare Act 2006. However, the legislation dates back to the 1930s.

By section 11, it is illegal to sell an animal to any person the seller has reasonable cause to believe is under the age of 16 years. It is also illegal to enter into an arrangement with a person under the age of 16 years which could result in the person winning an animal as a prize, unless the person is accompanied by a person over the age of 16 years.

The penalty for a breach is a maximum fine of £2,500 and/or imprisonment for up to 51 weeks.

Although there are provisions for disqualification from dealing in animals contained within the Act, these do not apply to offences of selling animals to under age purchasers. However, if it is considered that the act of selling the animal caused, or was likely to cause, unnecessary suffering to the animal, then the provisions disqualifying the seller from dealing in animals would be available to the courts.

9.9      Credit

The supply of credit, credit cards, hire agreements and loans is strictly regulated.

A person under the age of 18 years has no capacity to enter into a legally binding credit agreement, hire agreement, credit card or loan. The effect of this is that the debt is strictly unenforceable. For obvious reasons, therefore, credit and hire companies go to significant lengths to avoid entering into any agreements with any person under the age of 18.

It is also an offence to market credit facilities to persons under the age of 18 years, although as a result of case law (see below), this provision is now practically unenforceable. It is illegal to send a document to a person under 18 years of age inviting them to borrow money, obtain goods on credit or hire, obtain services on credit, apply for information or advice about credit.

It is a defence to show that the offender did not believe the person to be under 18 years of age. The defence does not apply if the document is sent to a school.

The prosecution must prove that not only has the defendant sent to a minor a document inviting him to borrow money, but that when so doing the defendant carried out that act with a view to financial gain[6]. The Alliance & Leicester Building Society, which sent a child a leaflet advertising loans, was not guilty of sending a minor a document inviting him to borrow money with a view to financial gain, because the leaflet specified that loans were not available to applicants under the age of 18.

The minor, aged 9, had had a savings account with the building society. With his annual statement he had received a mailshot which purported to offer up to £7,500 by way of an unsecured personal loan.

The justices had found that it was the building society's policy not to grant loans to persons under the age of 18, that its computer programme was written so as to prevent loans being granted to minors and that there were, at the bottom

---

[6] *Alliance & Leicester Building Society v Babbs* (1993) 157 JP 706

of one of the leaflet's 12 pages, the words 'Loans are not available to applicants under 18 years of age'. However, the justices had concluded that the building society was guilty of the offence because the leaflet had been sent to account holders regardless of their age and every invitation to borrow money had been, subject to company policy, with a view to financial gain.

In the judgement of the court, the document had to be read as a whole, including the words 'Loans are not available to applicants under 18 years of age'. When the document was so read it had to be construed as one whose operation was excluded to those under 18. The prosecution therefore fell at the first hurdle; the document was not an invitation to a minor, let alone to borrow money. Furthermore, the prosecution also failed at the second hurdle proving that the document was sent 'with a view to financial gain'.

The prosecution had argued that the building society had indiscriminately circulated all account holders and therefore the court should infer that it was the company's intention, where possible, to obtain applications whether from persons under or over 18 and therefore to obtain financial gain.

However, the fact that indiscriminate mail-shots of that kind were to be condemned did not mean that the building society was in breach of the 1974 Act.

Structures had existed which sought to eliminate minors from being granted loans, therefore it seemed that the only logical inference was that when the building society had sent the brochure out, it was not its intention to obtain financial gain from any person who received it that was a minor.

The effect of this case was that, contrary to what the Act actually says, it is unlikely to be an offence for a lender to send 'an invitation to apply' for credit to a minor as opposed to a 'pre-screened offer to apply' for credit. The difference is important.

An 'invitation to apply' is exactly that. The lender is extending an offer in a minor's name to apply for an account, but no credit history review has been done. It may be associated with a savings account opened in a minor's name, especially if the lender does not have a date of birth associated with the account. Or the advert may come as a result of the minor being on another type of membership list, such as a frequent flier list, which could cause a company to invite them to check out their services.

A 'pre-screened offer' is extended after a credit history review has been conducted and the individual meets the lender's qualifications for the extension of credit. If the credit history does not change by the time the minor responds to the offer, then the minor is approved. If the minor receives a pre-screened or pre-selected offer it would suggest a credit history has been established using their identifying information. This would be likely to still be an offence under the Act, but this type of open-ended offer is rare in UK credit advertising.

9.10   Necessary Goods

By section 3(2) of the Sale of Goods Act 1979, a contract with a minor (under the age of 18 years) is unenforceable unless it was for necessary goods. If it is, the minor is required to pay a reasonable price. The contract is enforceable by the minor to assert their other statutory rights against the seller. Necessary goods means goods suitable to the condition in life of the minor and to his actual requirements at the time of the sale and delivery.

The definition of necessaries includes obvious purchases, such as food and clothing, but also services or goods which are in furtherance of education or apprenticeship. The necessaries of one minor will not necessarily reflect those of another. The particular circumstances, such as age and immediate needs, may lead to differing outcomes. For example, in *Peters v Fleming*[7], it was found that a gold ring and watch chain were necessaries, for the child of a Member of Parliament. However, a contract may not be for necessaries where a minor's needs are adequately satisfied, or a purchase can be seen as unnecessary. This is demonstrated by *Nash v Inman*[8], where a tailor's claim that a child's purchase of 11 waistcoats was for necessaries failed, on the grounds that he already owned adequate clothing.

Although it is clear that contracts for necessaries can legally bind minors, the terms of such a contract may defeat it. Where a contract contains particularly burdensome or unfair terms, the courts may decide that a minor does not have the capacity to be bound by them. Where a minor hired a car and crashed it through no fault of his own, the owner could not recover his losses on the grounds that a contract term put the car entirely at the minor's risk[9].

By section 3 of the Minors Contracts Act 1987, a minor may be ordered by the court, if it is just and equitable to do so, to transfer the property acquired by the minor under the unenforceable or repudiated contract back to the seller.

---

[7] (1840) 151 ER 314
[8] [1902] 2 KB 1
[9] *Fawcett v Smethurst* (1914) 84 LJ KB 473

9.11    Social Networking

In the last 10 years the impact of social networking has expanded exponentially, with considerable concerns being raised by pressure groups about the impact on children. Most social networking sites require their users to be at least 13 years of age, but, at present, this is an entirely voluntary restriction. There are no laws in the UK imposing an age restriction on the use of social networking sites.

However, on 25th January 2012, the European Commission published its long awaited review of the data protection framework[10]. This proposal, if adopted, will implement new directly applicable laws on all member states regarding offering information society services to children. By proposed Article 8 (1) of the Regulation, it will only be lawful to process the personal data of a child below the age of 13 years if and to the extent that consent is given or authorised by the child's parent or custodian. The providers of information society services will be required to make reasonable efforts to obtain verifiable consent and the proposed Regulation provides for further Directives on how that might be achieved.

This Regulation, if adopted by the European Union, will effectively make social networking providers liable if users under the age of 13 are on their networks without their parent's consent. On 28th January 2015, EU Justice Commissioner Věra Jourová provided an update on negotiations to implement the Regulation and described it as a priority for 2015. It is envisaged that the Regulation will come into force by 2017/8.

9.12    Mobile Telephone or other 'Pay Monthly' Contracts

Mobile telephones and other devices, such as smartphones, tablet PCs or personal digital assistants (PDAs) are increasing popular for children. There is no legal minimum age for selling a mobile device to a young person, but there are some practical hurdles which effectively create a minimum age of 18 years for pay monthly contracts or SIM only contracts. There are fewer restrictions on pay as you go or 'top-up' devices, but there remain identification issues.

If a mobile telephone can be described as 'necessary goods' for the child (which is subject to some debate), the law will permit them to enter into a contract to

---

[10] COM (2012) 11 Proposal for a Regulation of the European Parliament and of the Council on the protection of individuals with regard to the processing of personal data and on the free movement of such data (General Data Protection Regulation) – Official Journal 25.1.12

purchase the goods[11]. For pay-as-you-go deals, the customer purchases the device outright and then pays to buy 'credit' or 'time' as and when they need it. There is generally no on-going commitment on the part of the customer. However, with 'pay monthly' or 'SIM only' contracts, the customer agrees to pay a monthly fee, usually for a minimum term and often in return for a heavily discounted or even free device. The company recoups the cost of the device over the course of the minimum term of the contract. In these cases, a check with a credit reference agency is required and production of a credit or debit card. The practical effect of this is to place a minimum age restriction of 18 years on these contracts.

In addition, all of the UK mobile telephone operators have agreed to a code of practice requiring them to take reasonable and practical steps to verify that a customer is 18 or over. This is for the purpose of enabling the mobile operator to implement appropriate content controls. There are two bodies that are responsible for the self-regulation of content services delivered over the mobile telephone network.

- Phonepay Plus is a co-regulatory body that has responsibility for the regulation of premium rate services delivered over electronic communications networks. Their code of practice can be found at www.phonepayplus.org.uk.
- Independent Mobile Classification Body is a self-regulatory body that determines whether or not content delivered through mobile operators networks should be classified as suitable for age 18 or over only. Their code of practice can be found at www.imcb.org.uk.

9.13   Clinical Trials

It is an offence to give an incentive or financial inducement to a person under the age of 16 years to participate in a clinical trial[12]. All clinical trials in the UK are administered under the Medicines for Human Use (Clinical Trials) Regulations 2004, which are made under section 2(2) of the European Communities Act 1972 as they implement the in the UK, European Clinical Trials Directive 2001/20/EC (EUCTD) to establish standardisation of research activity in clinical trials throughout the European Community.

Provision is allowed to be made for compensation for injury or loss. There is a defence available of taking all reasonable precautions and exercising all due diligence to avoid the offence. Unusually, by Regulation 51(2), where evidence

---

[11] S.3(2) Sale of Goods Act 1979
[12] Regulation 28(1) & 49(1), Medicines for Human Use (Clinical Trials) Regulations 2004 (SI2004:1031)

is presented demonstrating due diligence, the burden of disproving the defence is reversed to the prosecution, who must prove a lack of reasonable precautions or due diligence beyond reasonable doubt.

The penalty for non-compliance is unlimited and/or imprisonment for up to 3 months on conviction in a Magistrates' Court, an unlimited fine and/or imprisonment for up to 2 years, or both, on conviction in a Crown Court

These Regulations are enforced in the UK by the Medicines and Healthcare Products Regulatory Agency (MHRA). The authorisation process and medical ethics committees for clinical trials have powers under the Regulations to impose stricter restrictions on individual trials.

9.14     Teeth Whitening Products

The use of strong teeth whitening products on persons under 18 is prohibited by R.12(1) of the Cosmetic Products Enforcement Regulations 2013[13].
This is a complex offence to describe.

Schedule 4 to the 2013 Regulations prohibits breach of safety regulations or restrictions on substance use set out within the EU Cosmetic Products Regulations[14] which include restrictions around any:

"Hydrogen peroxide and other compounds or mixtures that release hydrogen peroxide, including carbamide peroxide and zinc peroxide tooth whitening or bleaching products  which contain > 0.1 % ≤ 6 % of H2O2, present or released"

These products are only sold to dental practitioners, for each cycle of use, first use by dental practitioners or under their direct supervision if an equivalent level of safety is ensured. Afterwards the product can be provided to the consumer to complete the cycle of use. The product must not be used on a person under 18 years of age.

So this is the age restricted element, but it is not an offence to use it as such – it is a composition offence - it is an offence for a tooth whitening product to

---

[13]  (SI2013:1478)
[14] The EU Regulation was amended by COMMISSION REGULATION (EU) No 344/2013 of 4 April 2013 amending Annexes II, III, V and VI to Regulation (EC) No 1223/2009 of the European Parliament and of the Council on cosmetic products

contain > 0.1% of H2O2 if it is used on an under 18. The offence is if the product contains more than 0.1 % – the cosmetic product itself (the tooth whitening product) can be seized. The offence would be committed by the 'responsible person' i.e. the dental practitioner. It is likely that action would be taken by the General Dental Council against such an errant practitioner.

Notwithstanding this, teeth whitening services are often made available in beauty salons by unregistered practitioners (which is an offence), but it is not entirely clear if they would also be committing the offence of supplying the teeth whitening product to a person under 18 as they could not be a 'responsible person' under the terms of the Regulations.

Trading Standards Officers have extensive powers of enforcement under the 2013 Regulations. The penalty for breaching these provisions is an unlimited fine and/or up to three months imprisonment before Magistrates or up to one year's imprisonment before the Crown Court or both.

There is a statutory defence available of taking all reasonable steps and exercising all due diligence to avoid committing the offence.

9.15    Local Restrictions (including Voluntary Restrictions)

Many businesses impose their own voluntary restrictions on goods which are not otherwise age restricted by legislation. This is based on the principle that a shop owner is not obliged to sell goods on display in their store to anyone who is willing to pay for them[15].

Common goods that fall into this category include:

- Household chemicals
- Matches, lighters, firelighters and lighter fuel
- High energy drinks
- Eggs and flour (particularly around Halloween where children use them for mischief)
- Adult magazines, explicit newspapers

---

[15] *Pharmaceutical Society of Great Britain v Boots Cash Chemists (Southern) Ltd* [1953] 1 QB 401

CHAPTER TEN

# REASONABLE PRECAUTIONS AND DUE DILIGENCE

## CONTENTS

10.1    Introduction

Many consumer law statutes create strict liability offences in which the lack of necessity for the prosecution to prove guilty knowledge is offset by a statutory defence. Such defences typically contain at least two common elements which require the defendant to prove firstly that he took 'all reasonable precautions' and, secondly, that he 'exercised all due diligence', in each case, to avoid the commission of the offence. The two elements together are often referred to as 'the due diligence defence'.

This approach is adopted in many, but importantly not all, age restricted goods legislation. Some statutes refer to 'all reasonable steps' rather than to 'all reasonable precautions' but there is no practical difference in the meaning of these two terms.

10.2    Summary of Reasonable Precautions and Due Diligence

The due diligence defence which has given rise to the most judicial consideration is that contained in S.24(1) of the Trade Descriptions Act 1968, which is outside the scope of this book. However, the general principles that are applied in cases under other legislation are also applied to cases under age restricted sales legislation, so it is necessary to examine some of those cases.

The leading case on the exercise of reasonable precautions and due diligence in companies is *Tesco Supermarkets Ltd v Nattrass*[1]. In that case, the company alleged that the offence (a pricing offence) was due to the act or default of a store manager and that the company itself had taken all reasonable precautions and exercised all due diligence to avoid the commission of the offence. Viscount Dilhorne said:

> '*That an employer, whether a company or an individual, may reasonably appoint someone to secure that the obligations imposed by the Act are observed cannot be doubted. ... He cannot excuse himself if the person appointed fails to do what he is supposed to do unless he can show that he himself has taken [all reasonable]*

---

[1] [1972] AC 153

*precautions and exercised [all due] diligence. Whether or not he has done so is a question of fact and while it may be that the appointment of a competent person amounts in the circumstances of a particular case to the taking of all reasonable precautions, if he does nothing after making the appointment to see that proper steps are in fact being taken to comply with the Act, it cannot be said that he has exercised all due diligence.'*

Lord Diplock, similarly, said:

*'If ... the principal is able to identify a person to whose act or default the offence was actually due, he still has to show that he himself exercised due diligence to devise an effective system to avoid such acts or defaults on the part of his servants and to satisfy himself that such system was being observed. ... If the principal has taken all reasonable precautions in the selection and training of servants to perform supervisory duties and has laid down an effective system of supervision and used due diligence to see that it is observed, he is entitled to rely on a default by a superior servant in his supervisory duties as a defence under S.24(1), as well as, or instead of, on an act or default of an inferior servant who has no supervisory duties under his contract of employment.'*

The House of Lords thus made a distinction between 'precautions' and 'diligence' so that, in the context of an employer setting up an effective system to ensure compliance with the Act, the system is the precaution and the monitoring of it is the diligence.

A defendant need only show that he took all *reasonable* precautions and exercised all *due* diligence. If there was nothing that could reasonably have been expected to be done then to do nothing could on rare occasions be reasonable[2]. In nearly all cases, however, there will be at least one reasonable thing which could have been done to avoid the commission of the offence. If one or more things can be identified, then systems have to be put in place to address them. The systems do not have to be fool-proof, but they do have to be reasonable[3]. This chapter sets out some of the precautions that are considered to be reasonable, but each case must be determined on its own merits.

---

[2] *Hurley v Martinez & Co* Ltd (1990) 154 JP 821
[3] *Texas Homecare Ltd v Stockport MBC* (1988) 152 JP 83

The courts have distinguished the principles in *Tesco v Nattrass* where the available statutory defence imputes knowledge on the part of the offender, as is the case under s.11(2) of the Video Recordings Act 1984. In another case involving Tesco, the court held that as their management could not be expected to have any knowledge or information as to the age of a casual purchaser of a video film, the relevant factor was the knowledge or reasonable grounds for belief of the employee involved in the transaction. There was no statutory distinction drawn between Tesco and those under its control.[4]

Tightening up systems following a failed test purchase does not necessarily undermine the reasonableness of the precautions that were in place at the time of the offence. It is a question of fact for magistrates to consider[5].

In *Davies v Carmarthenshire CC*[6] the court considered the systems and procedures adopted by the defendant to be of considerable importance to the application of the due diligence defence. These included:

- That the sales assistant in question had been provided with written material designed to prevent under age sales
- That there had been prominent display throughout the store of the supermarket's policy of requesting age identification from anyone who looked under 21 years old before selling alcohol to them
- That the tills at the supermarket were fitted with a device designed to prevent under age sales of alcohol by requiring a sales assistant to be satisfied of an individual's age before a sale of alcohol could be effected, and
- That there were records of previous occasions when the assistant had refused to sell alcohol to a person because she believed that the individual was underage.

The application of the statutory defence is a question of fact for Magistrates and provided their conclusion is not perverse, the higher courts are unlikely to alter their findings[7].

10.3    Age Verification and the Proof of Age Standards Scheme

Effective age verification systems and procedures are the cornerstone of the

---

[4] *Tesco Stores Ltd v Brent LBC* [1993] 2 All ER 718 and *Smith v T&S Stores PLC* (1995) 14 Tr. L. R. 337
[5] *London Borough of Enfield v Argos Ltd* [2008] EWHC 2598
[6] [2005] EWHC 464
[7] Hereford & Worcester CC v T&S Stores PLC (1994) 93LGR98

reasonable precautions and due diligence defence. Official guidance varies, but generally accepted good practice is that age verification should be undertaken by reference to one of three sorts of official documentation:

- A UK Driver and Vehicle Licensing Agency issued photocard driving licence
- A UK Identity and Passport Service issued passport
- An identity card bearing a PASS hologram

Retailers should take particular care to verify the holder of the card matches the customer and to identify the correct date on the card as being that date of birth. This can be particularly difficult on the driving licence and passport as a number of different dates are shown on the face of the document. It is not recommended that overseas driving licences or passports are accepted because it would be difficult for shop workers who are unfamiliar with the genuine articles to identify a fraudulent one[8].

The Proof of Age Standards Scheme (PASS) is the UK's national proof of age accreditation scheme, endorsed by the Home Office, the Association of Chief Police Officers (ACPO), the Security Industry Authority (SIA) and the Trading Standards Institute (TSI). In June 2014, the PASS Board approved a new unified design, which applies to all cards except the Young Scot card. This provides an opportunity to standardise training and improve recognition of the cards by retailers and security staff.

PASS sets and maintains minimum criteria for all proof of age card issuers to meet. All cards schemes are required to submit to periodic audits carried out by an independent audit team appointed by the Trading Standards Institute (TSI) to ensure that they meet and keep the standards required for PASS accreditation.

The aim of PASS is to provide:
- Reliability
- Assurance
- Confidence for retailers, enforcers and young people

The PASS hologram on a card is the hallmark indicating that the card issuer has passed a stringent audit carried out by Trading Standards Officers and that the card may be relied upon. As a part of due diligence procedures, sellers of age

---

[8] This might not apply to outlets serving particular immigrant communities where the staff are familiar with the official identify documents of that community.

restricted goods are encouraged to accept PASS accredited cards as proof-of-age. There are many local schemes, but three main national schemes – CitizenCard, Validate and Young Scot.

In 2008, the Retail of Alcohol Standards Group (RASG) set up the 'Challenge 21' and 'Challenge 25' schemes, which aim to put a 'buffer' between the restricted age and the age at which to challenge for verification.

In the *London Borough of Enfield v Argos Ltd* [9], Moses LJ said:

> *'I would regard a policy that required members of staff to aim considerably higher than the age prohibited by statute as a reasonable and sensible one.'*

The scheme operates by saying that if a person appears to be under the age of 25, they will be expected to produce identification to prove that they are over the age of 18. RASG have produced a series of royalty-free posters promoting the scheme, which are now widely used in retail premises throughout the UK.

In some local licensing areas, conditions have been added to licenses making a 'Challenge 25' scheme a mandatory requirement. In theory, this would mean that if a person aged 18 – 25 entered the store to purchase alcohol and they were not challenged for ID, an offence of breach of a licence condition could be established. However, it would depend on the exact wording of the condition and the public policy arguments about making a voluntary precaution a mandatory requirement leading to liability for another offence. That remains to be tested in the courts.

## 10.4   Staff Training

A critical precaution to avoid under age sales is to ensure that staff are properly trained and equipped with the skills to verify the age of purchasers. This training must be adequate and kept up to date.

There is a BTEC Vocational Qualification available in preventing under age sales. This is a nationally recognised qualification and is available as face to face training, distance learning workbooks or e-learning options. Further information on all of the various options and current providers of this training can be found at www.underagesales.co.uk.

---

[9] [2008] EWHC 2598

In addition, some local authorities have developed their own bespoke training programmes and there is a national module called *Do you PASS?* linked to the Fair Trading Award. Further information about this module and how to contact local trading standards services about whether or not they provide their own training can be found at www.tradingstandards.uk.

Particular care needs to be taken with providers offering 'online' training solutions. If they are not BTEC accredited or provided by Trading Standards Departments, they should be viewed with suspicion and they are unlikely to satisfy the requirements for adequate official training.

10.5    Store Layout and Signage

Careful consideration needs to be given to the layout of stores and, in particular, where age restricted products are placed. If possible, they should be placed behind the counter. However, if they are placed on general display, as is often the case with alcohol, they ought to be kept together and within sight of the tills or supervision. The risk of displaying items in a piecemeal, confused or cavalier way, may lead to confusion in the minds of staff members about which goods are age restricted or not[10].

In some cases, local licensing conditions have restricted the availability of alcohol within stores. In *Tesco v Licensing Justices for the Petty Sessional Division of Mold*[11] the Crown Court dismissed Tesco's appeal against the decision of the Licensing Justices to impose a requirement that the alcohol be within a defined area and demarcation from other goods. The court said:

> *"That the prime consideration must be the prevention of the sale of alcohol to those under-age. This was more easily achieved by the method of a "shop within a shop" than by the sale of alcohol alongside other goods in the store without demarcation. The control of alcohol sales by reference to supervisors overseeing the operation of the tills was felt to be inadequate."*

Some store signage is mandatory – in particular:

- The statutory tobacco notice required under section 4(1) of the Children and Young Persons (Protection from Tobacco) Act 1991 (see chapter 3.7, ante)
- The statutory fireworks notice required under Regulation 10(1) of the Fireworks Regulations 2004 (see chapter 7.7, ante)

---

[10] *London Borough of Croydon v Pinch-a-Pound* [2010] EWHC 3283 (Admin)
[11] *Tesco v Licensing Justices for the Petty Sessional Division of Mold* [1989] C.L.Y. 2267

Signage may occasionally be required by virtue of imposed licensing conditions on individual licences. Common conditions can include a requirement to post notices concerning the 'Challenge 25' scheme.

Failure to show statutory notices or notices required by conditions on licences is an offence under the relevant legislation. However, failure to display other warning notices may be considered to be an absent reasonable precaution and, hence, negate an available statutory defence.

There are many sources of signage, but in 2008 the Retail of Alcohol Standards Group launched new standard signage for the 'Challenge 25' scheme. This signage is available to download and use royalty-free from the Wine and Spirit Trade Association website (www.wsta.co.uk).

## 10.6    Technology, including CCTV and E-POS Systems

### 10.6.1    Closed Circuit Television

CCTV systems can help to reduce the incidence of under age sales and improve the security of retail premises. They also provide a surveillance opportunity for restricted goods kept away from the counter. To be effective, CCTV should be mostly overt, with adequate signage and coverage both inside and outside the store. Some licensed premises may have specific conditions concerning CCTV on their licence.

Any premises owner considering the installation of CCTV is advised to make contact with their local Crime Prevention Officer, who usually works for the local police or council. They will advise on the appropriate CCTV system to install and may have access to additional support funding for CCTV installations, although this is less common in recent years. Some suggestions for camera locations include areas with a high risk of violence or stock loss, all entry and exit points from inside and outside, cash offices or storerooms, outdoor areas such as gardens or car parks, counter areas, separate rooms where visibility from counters or bars is hindered, and toilet areas (but not inside the toilets).

CCTV is not a panacea to tackling the problem of under age sales or work related violence; it must be used in combination with other prevention methods. It is important that all staff know how to use the CCTV system, operate the cameras (if they have pan-tilt-zoom capability) and have appropriate training, which may include a need for authorisation by the Security Industry Authority (depending on the size, type and usage of the CCTV systems).

The recorded footage should be kept for a minimum of 14 days, but ideally for 31 days. If the CCTV system is digital, the cost of image storage is now very small in comparison with the cost of the system itself.

The quality of CCTV may be worse at lower light levels. Some cameras are also unable to cope with or adapt to artificial lighting, neon lighting, low lighting, street lighting or lighting that is too close in the hours of darkness. This can lead to strobing or glare and affects the ability to monitor images and the quality of recorded images.

A visible CCTV monitor is a useful deterrent, but care needs to be taken with the images shown on public display monitors. In general, if the image is one that the viewer could see by merely looking from where they are stood, it will be fine. However, if the image shows a private area that the viewer would not normally have access to, such as stock rooms, this can be problematic and may reduce the security of that private area.

Anyone that operates a CCTV system is required to notify the Information Commissioner about what information is recorded and the purpose for doing so (www.ico.gov.uk).

10.6.2   Electronic Point-of-Sale

E-POS (Electronic Point of Sale) is the system used to enable price look up (PLU) from a barcode or other identifier on a product. Nearly all consumer products carry a barcode with a unique identifier, called an International Article Number or EAN[12].

A standard EAN is 13 digits long, but smaller EAN-8 numbers are available for goods with limited packaging space and longer EAN-2 and EAN-5 suffixes (in addition to the EAN-13 number) are available for goods like periodicals or newspapers to denote issue numbers.

The EAN provides an opportunity for restrictions to be placed on individual products or classes of products and most E-POS systems now provide an age screening module to protect against under age sales. It is important for sellers of restricted goods to ensure that this system is activated, although it may be permissible to deactivate it in circumstances where 100% of sales are age restricted, such as dedicated tobacco kiosks.

---

[12] This used to be called an European Article Number, hence "EAN", but is now called an International Article Number although the "EAN" code was retained.

The scanning of the EAN should cause the E-POS system to prompt to the till operative that the product is age restricted and give an indication of the age restriction in place. The better systems also provide the latest date of birth that a purchaser needs to be in order to legally purchase the goods. In addition, the better systems provide a series of options such as 'approved', 'decline – no ID', 'decline – invalid ID', 'decline – proxy sale', etc. This can then ameliorate the need for a separate paper refusals register.

### 10.6.3   Biometric Verification Systems

There are a number of different biometric identification systems available for use. These systems typically rely upon initial verification of an official document, such as a passport, associated with a biometric feature, such as a fingerprint.

These systems are increasingly popular for on-licensed premises like pubs and clubs, but are available for all different sorts of age restricted products.

## 10.7   Product Marking

The overt or covert marking of products is often cited as a reasonable precaution, although the provenance of this is untested. It is probably more likely to be a useful tool for law enforcement to trace the origin of restricted products when they are found in the possession of young people. It does not, of course, follow that an illegal sale has taken place, as it may be the result of 'proxy purchasing'. Nevertheless, licensing authorities have imposed conditions on licences that require covert or overt product marking.

If it is required, it can be achieved in many ways. Overt marking might include, for instance, an individual price label with the store's logo on that is to be applied to each product. This might be considered onerous, especially where stores are using electronic point-of-sale equipment with price look-up capability.

Covert marking is more commonly undertaken in consultation with the police. It might require the retailer to mark products with a particular colour of ultra-violet pen. This is again onerous for retailers. There are covert marking sprays that are generally available and which can be used to spray ultra-violet markers onto products. If using any kind of covert marking, particularly sprays, care needs to be taken to ensure that areas that may come into contact with the alcohol inside the packaging are not contaminated. Covert marking sprays are generally not tested or approved as an article for contact with food and so spraying the tops of cans or bottles should be avoided.

10.8    Record Keeping

Records are an important part of a due diligence defence. Although law enforcement officers are generally more concerned with the reality of the training or systems that are in place, if a retailer does not have adequate records then this can undermine their defence and indicate a lack of 'due diligence' in their approach.

It is important that records are kept neat, tidy and together, so a designated file is usually advisable. Larger companies have detailed age restriction systems and procedures dictated by head office. Smaller stores may have their own ad hoc records or may rely on one of the 'off-the-shelf' diligence files that are generally available.

Records ought to include, as a minimum:

- The formal Age Verification Policy
- A list of all of the age restricted products that the store sells and their location
- A list of all staff authorised to sell age restricted products
- A copy of their initial training (ideally externally accredited) and a record of all refresher training
- Any letters confirming the outcome of test purchase operations (either from law enforcement, the National Lottery operator or self-instructed test purchases)

10.9    Effective Diligence, Audit and Review

Any reasonable precaution system must be kept under continuous review to ensure that it is working effectively to achieve its objectives. This review is the 'due diligence' aspect of the defence.

The level and extent of audit will depend upon what is reasonable in the circumstances, but might include:

- Observing staff undertaking restricted sales
- Reviewing transaction logs, CCTV and the refusals register
- Speaking to staff to see if they remain aware of the rules and policies in place
- Checking to see that all appropriate signage is still in place, legible and visible

In addition, there are companies that provide test purchasing services for retailers to provide an external verification of the systems in place. The results of these can be valuable evidence of effective due diligence.

Any review or audit should be recorded with the results, positive or negative. It is accepted that mistakes happen; law enforcement are interested in what lessons are learnt from mistakes, what systems and procedures are in place and whether or not, in general, they are working well.

As final reassurance, it is recommended that retailers obtain an external audit of compliance and have this certified. For more information about this, visit www.underagesales.co.uk.

10.10   Scalability of 'Reasonable'

What might be reasonable for a large national chain would not necessarily be reasonable for a village shop. What is reasonable will vary from case to case and will depend in part on the proportionality of the costs involved and the size of the defendant's organisation.  In the *Tesco Stores Ltd v Nattrass*[13], Lord Diplock said:

> *'What the employer or principal can reasonably be expected to do to prevent the commission of an offence will depend on the gravity of the injury which it is sought to prevent and the nature of the business in the course of which such offences are committed. ... If considerations of cost and business practicability did not play a part in determining what employers carrying on such businesses could reasonably be expected to do to prevent the commission of an offence under the Act, the price to the public of the protection afforded to a minority of consumers might well be an increase in the cost of goods and services to customers generally.'*

In *Garrett v Boots The Chemists Ltd* [14], where Boots sold pencils with an excessive metallic lead and chromium content, Lane LCJ said:

> *'What might be reasonable for a large retailer might not be reasonable for the village shop. But here, dealing with a concern the size of Boots, it seems to me that one of the obvious precautions to be taken was a random sample, whether statistically controlled or*

---

[13] [1972] AC 153
[14] (1980) 88 ITSA MR 238

*not. One does not know whether the random sample would have in fact produced detection of the errant pencils. It might have, it might not have. But to say that it was not a precaution which should reasonably have been taken does not seem to me to accord with good sense.'*

## 10.11   Internet Sales

Online trading presents particular challenges for age verification. With a remote customer, visual verification of their age is not possible, but the age restrictions on the supply of goods continue to apply.

Retailers are still required to take reasonable steps to verify a purchaser's age online. The most practical minimum step that can be taken is to insist on payment by credit card. Credit cards require the holder to be 18, so restricting the sales of all age restricted goods to credit card holders is both a simple and effective way of verifying the purchaser's age. Debit cards do not provide the same assurance. There are a number of pre-paid debit cards available to those under 18 and a number of ordinary debit cards such as Visa, Maestro, Solo and Electron can be legitimately held by under 18s. Some of these cards are offered to children as young as 11.

Age verification checks at the point of delivery may be an option, however this will usually be impractical as the consumers may be out. Also, couriers are a third party and may not be happy to accept responsibility for age verification so probably won't be able to be relied upon as a defence. Larger companies, with adequate resources, carry out more detailed checks using the electoral register and/or credit reference agencies. The checks can be done quickly, in the time it takes to make a card transaction.

For a small number of national companies who have the appropriate facilities, it is possible for the customer to be able only to view and reserve the age restricted products on their website, and then collect the items in person from a store. The website has a message that states 'Due to age restrictions on the sale of this product, it is only possible to reserve the item for store pick-up (must be over 18)'. Staff must be trained to verify the age and check ID when the product is collected, as they would do in a normal shop.

There are some practices that are unlikely to be regarded as taking 'reasonable precautions' and, thus, will not assist a retailer in defending against unlawful sales. These include:

- Using a general disclaimer such as 'Anyone ordering a [product] from our website will be deemed to be at least 18 years of age'
- Website statements that the company will only supply to over 18s or that a consumer commits an offence if they are under 18
- Tick-boxes that the customer must complete to state that they are over 18 or providing a date of birth are not sufficient, even if an e-mail or letter is sent to the purchaser to confirm their age. However, it is good practice to flag up goods which have an age restriction and ask a customer to confirm their age, as long as you are not relying on this completely as your system for age checks
- Offering to take payment methods that do not require a customer to be 18 such as Visa Delta, cheque or postal order
- Some websites offer e-payment services such as PayPal, Nochex or Wordpay. These services may require a customer to be over 18, but they may not verify a user's age

Any effective prevention system for supplying age restricted goods online is likely to have at least one element that does not rely on information or assurances provided by the buyer.

There are a number of specialist companies providing online age verification services.

10.12   Duress

The defence of duress in criminal law is where a defendant admits breaking the law, but claims that they were overwhelmed by some threatened or actual harm. The threat of violence is often cited as a reason why age restricted sales take place, but it is extremely unlikely to be an available defence during a prosecution. This is because the vast majority of prosecutions are based upon test purchases conducted under police or trading standards supervision which, by its nature, does not involve threats of violence.

The basis of the defence is that the duress actually overwhelmed the defendant's will and would have overwhelmed the will of a person of ordinary courage, thus rendering the entire behaviour involuntary.

In *R v Graham*[15], the Lord Chief Justice set out the test for a defence of duress to succeed:

---

[15] [1981] EWCA Crim 5

'As a matter of public policy, it seems to us essential to limit the defence of duress by means of an objective criterion formulated in terms of reasonableness. Consistency of approach in defences to criminal liability is obviously desirable. Provocation and duress are analogous. In provocation the words or actions of one person break the self-control of another. In duress the words or actions of one person break the will of another. The law requires a defendant to have the self-control reasonably to be expected of the ordinary citizen in his situation. It should likewise require him to have the steadfastness reasonably to be expected of the ordinary citizen in his situation. So too with self-defence, in which the law permits the use of no more force than is reasonable in the circumstances. And, in general, if a mistake is to excuse what would otherwise be criminal, the mistake must be a reasonable one.'

In general, although it is a matter of individual merits, it is highly unlikely that a defence of duress would be available to a charge relating to age restricted sales.

CHAPTER ELEVEN

# POWERS OF LAW ENFORCEMENT OFFICERS

## CONTENTS

## 11.1    Trading Standards Officers

Trading Standards Officers (TSO's) are the principal, but not exclusive, law enforcement officers for age restrictions in England and Wales. They are employed by upper tier local authorities, that is, in England and Wales:

- County Councils
- London Boroughs and the Corporation of London
- Metropolitan Boroughs
- Unitary Authorities
- Welsh County Boroughs

Normally, TSO's have extensive powers of enforcement, but these powers are significantly reduced for the majority of age restricted sales legislation. In fact, only restrictions on fireworks and cigarette lighter refills carry TSO's 'normal' powers of enforcement by virtue of the fact that they are safety regulations under the Consumer Protection Act 1987.

This does not mean, however, that TSOs are powerless to act if under age sales are suspected and the most common enforcement tool used by them is the use of test purchase volunteers. This is where a young person under the relevant age is used to purchase or attempt to purchase the restricted goods. Usually, but not universally, the young person is exempted from the commission of any offence where this is the case.

Where a young person is acting as an agent of a TSO or a local authority, the test purchase is still deemed to have been completed even though the property in the goods may transfer to the local authority rather than the test purchaser[1].

## 11.2    Police Officers

Police officers are also actively engaged in age restricted sales enforcement. They take a particular lead on the sale of weapons, such as firearms, air weapons, knives and explosives.

---

[1] *Wm Morrisons Supermarkets Plc v Reading BC* [2012] EWHC 1358 (Admin)

Their powers of enforcement derive from their general powers principally set out in the Police and Criminal Evidence Act 1984. In addition, some of the specific age restricted goods legislation provides them with additional powers of enforcement, particularly entry to premises without a warrant.

11.3   Other Law Enforcement Officers

Other active law enforcement officers in this field include:
- Local Licensing Authority officers – particularly since 25th April 2012, when they have acquired powers to bring Licensing Reviews on their own instigation
- Local community safety teams or anti-social behaviour officers
- Officers of the Gambling Commission
- Staff from the National Lottery operator (Operation Child)
- Monitoring (but generally not enforcement) by staff from the British Board of Film Classification and the Video Standards Council
- Officers of the Child Exploitation and Online Protection Centre (part of the Serious Organised Crime Agency)
- Medicines and Healthcare Products Regulatory Agency

11.4   Test Purchasing Code of Practice

In January 2013, the Government published a new code of practice for regulators on the enforcement of age restricted products and services legislation. This was updated in April 2014.

The original code of practice for test purchasing was published in 2002 by the former Local Authorities Coordinators of Regulatory Services (LACORS); it was an attempt to bring together the practice of the day and update the original Home Office guidance contained in circular 17/1992.

There have been a number of appeal cases concerning test purchase operations including:
- Teixeira de Castro v Portugal (1998) 28 EHRR 101
- Tesco Stores Limited v Brent LBC [1993] 2 All ER 718
- Hereford and Worcester County Council v T & S Stores Plc (1994) 93 LGR 98
- LB of Ealing v Woolworths Plc [1995] Crim LR 58
- R v Loosley Attorney Generals Ref.(No3 of 2000) [2002] 1 UKHL 53
- City of Sunderland Council v Dawson [2004] EWHC 2796 (Admin)
- Davies v Carmarthenshire County Council [2005] EWHC 464

Changes in particular to alcohol licensing legislation prompted a significant growth in the number of test purchase operations carried out by some local authorities and also encouraged partnership working with other organisations, most notably the police. Other significant changes include an increase in the availability and use of proof of age cards by young people, which again has an impact upon the nature of test purchase operations. There have also been a number of decided legal cases in this area.

The new code of practice published by the government's Better Regulation Delivery Office, is reproduced in full below. It is split into four sections:

A. Prioritisation
B. Working with businesses and communities
C. Conduct of checks on compliance
D. Responses to non-compliance

Age Restricted Products and Services: a Code of Practice for Regulatory Delivery

A) Prioritisation

**1.      An enforcing authority should understand and communicate the contribution that its regulatory activities in respect of age restricted products and services make to the outcomes that it is committed to delivering.**

Guidance:

1.1      A local authority's expressed outcomes are likely to include protecting young people from harm, keeping communities safe, and supporting vibrant business communities, all of which will be of relevance here.

1.2      Enforcing authorities could consider using a tool such as BRDO's Outcomes and Impacts Toolkit[2] to help them to demonstrate the impact of their regulatory activities in this area.

1.3      A local authority's annual determinations of the extent to which it will carry out a programme of enforcement activity in relation to tobacco products[3] and spray paints[4] provide it with an opportunity to articulate its outcomes, and the contribution that its enforcement activities will make to delivering those outcomes in respect of those products.

---

[2] Outcomes and Impacts Toolkit Summary, Local Better Regulation Office, 2010
[3] Children and Young Persons (Protection from Tobacco) Act 1991, section 5
[4] Anti-Social Behaviour Act 2003, s.54A

1.4   An annual service plan or business plan provides a mechanism for communicating the contribution that regulatory activities in this area make to the enforcing authority's outcomes, as do published standards and the authority's enforcement policy.[5]

1.5   A licensing authority's preparation and publication of its Licensing Policy[6] and its Statement of Principles[7] under the Gambling Act provide it with an opportunity to articulate its outcomes in respect of the protection of children from harm, and the contribution that its enforcement activities will make to delivering those outcomes.

**2.    An enforcing authority should ensure that its regulatory resources are allocated on the basis of an assessment of the priority risks in its area.**

Guidance:

2.1   An evidence-based approach will enable an enforcing authority to make informed decisions on what needs to be done and why, so that it can allocate the required resources. At this stage, the enforcing authority is not considering the targeting of individual businesses, but is making strategic decisions about its response to the most significant risks to its local community, including its local businesses. In considering relevant evidence, a local authority might ask itself, for example:

- What are the problems in our local area? What sources of information and data are available to us in addition to public complaints?
- Is there a high level of alcohol consumption by young people, and by under 15s in particular? This may be evidenced by high levels of anti-social behaviour or by high levels of alcohol-related hospital admissions for young people.
- Are smoking levels higher in some communities or groups than others? Youth smoking survey data, smoking prevalence data and visual sights of groups of young people smoking may indicate areas where youth smoking rates are high.
- Is graffiti in a particular area incurring costs for the local authority and local businesses? Are young people producing the graffiti?
- Is there a problem with street gangs in the area? Are there high levels of knife crime? Are there high levels of hospital admissions as a result of knife crime?
- Are online retailers based in your area a priority?

---

[5] Regulators' Code, section 6
[6] Licensing Act 2003, section 5
[7] Gambling Act 2006, section 349

2.2    Enforcing authorities should consider how they can best work with local communities to understand and tackle priority issues within those communities.

2.3    Not all age restricted products and services present the same level of potential harm. An enforcing authority's assessment will need to take into account the potential harm associated with non-compliance, as well as the likelihood of non-compliance.

**3.**    **An enforcing authority should work collaboratively with partner organisations that have shared outcomes, to tackle the risks identified. In particular:**

a)    **A local authority will want to consider its contribution to public health initiatives that focus on protecting young people from the harm associated with age restricted products such as alcohol and tobacco.**

b)    **Where enforcing authorities work with others who are involved in educating young people, they should promote awareness and use of the Age Restricted Products and Services Framework.**

c)    **Where a local authority and the police share enforcement responsibilities, they should co-ordinate their approach.**

d)    **Where a local authority and a national regulator (such as the Gambling Commission) share enforcement responsibilities, the local authority and the national regulator should co-ordinate their approach and should share information that will improve the targeting of resources and minimise any potential for duplication of effort.**

Guidance:

3.1    Tackling the problems associated with age restricted products and services requires a holistic approach, and involves collaborative working between a range of organisations. Some approaches will be best led by the enforcement agency, particularly where the focus is on the role that business plays, whilst some approaches will be led by other agencies, often with support from the enforcing authority.

3.2 Forums for co-ordinating activity might include:

- Crime and Disorder Reduction Partnerships;
- Local Alcohol Action Areas
- Responsible Authorities Working Groups;

---

[8] Further information available at www.communityalcoholpartnerships.co.uk

- Health and Wellbeing Boards;
- Community Alcohol Partnerships[8] and other retail and community initiatives
- Local Enterprise Partnerships;
- Business Improvement Districts;
- Town Centre Partnerships; and
- regional tobacco control groups.

3.3    Growing evidence[9] shows that age restricted products are often sourced by young people by routes other than traditional retail supplies. Community engagement and educational activities are sometimes more appropriate responses to issues such as proxy purchases by parents, friends and relatives, and illicit supplies, which can impact in areas where conventional enforcement activities are not appropriate.

B) Working with businesses and communities

**4.    Enforcing authorities should ensure that their compliance and enforcement approach to age restricted products and services legislation, including their approach to targeting their compliance and enforcement activities in this area, is transparent[10][11].**

Guidance:

4.1    The enforcing authority's service standards and enforcement policy should be published[12] and should be easily accessible to those that it regulates. For example, links to the policy would usually be made available on the enforcing authority's website.

4.2    The scope of the enforcing authority's enforcement policy should be clear, so that those regulated in relation to age restricted products and services legislation are able to easily identify that the policy is relevant to them.

4.3    Where an enforcing authority targets some or all of its compliance and enforcement activities on the basis of a nationally produced risk methodology, then it should make this known to those that it regulates, for example by

---

[9] See source material at Annex 1, Research and Project Evaluation on the BRDO website
[10] Legislative and Regulatory Reform Act 2006, section 21, requires relevant regulatory functions to be carried out in a way which is transparent.
[11] The Better Regulation Delivery Office has produced an example of approaches to developing service standards and an enforcement policy as part of its Regulators' Code Section 6: Local Authority Toolkit.
[12] Regulators' Code, section 6 (applicable to local authorities and to the Gambling Commission).

including a link to published details of the scheme in its compliance and enforcement policy, or elsewhere on its website.

4.4    Where an enforcing authority targets some or all of these activities on the basis of its own risk methodology, then it should involve those it regulates and other interested parties in designing this risk methodology, should publish details of it, and should review it regularly, taking into account any feedback provided by those it regulates and other interested parties[13].

**5.    An enforcing authority should select compliance and enforcement activities that offer the greatest opportunity to deliver improved outcomes for young people, local communities and businesses.**

Guidance:

5.1    An enforcing authority will usually have a wide range of options available to it, including: raising awareness of the legislation and compliance issues with business; providing advice and guidance to business; working through primary authorities; conducting checks on compliance; and dealing appropriately with compliance breaches, including taking swift and firm action where necessary.

5.2    In choosing the most appropriate option, the enforcing authority will need to think about the outcomes that it is trying to achieve, the public interest, and where its intervention, or an intervention by others, is likely to have the greatest impact[14].

**6.    An enforcing authority should ensure that clear information and guidance on relevant legislation are readily available to those that it regulates.**

Guidance:

6.1    Enforcing authorities will need to ensure[15], in particular, that:

- They provide appropriate means for businesses to seek and access compliance advice.
- Legal requirements are promptly communicated or made available to those regulated.

---

[13] Regulators' Code, sections 3 and 6
[14] See material at Annex 1, Research and Project Evaluation, including NHS Scotland's study of the impact of measures used to enforce underage alcohol sales regulations on the BRDO website.
[15] Regulators' Code, section 5

- General information, advice and guidance are provided in clear, concise and accessible language, using a range of appropriate formats and media.
- Compliance advice clearly distinguishes between statutory requirements and other advice or guidance. This section is of particular relevance in relation to age restricted products and services legislation, where much of the advice and guidance offered relates not to interpreting statutory requirements but to the controls that a business puts in place in order to meet those requirements.

6.2     An enforcing authority may choose to signpost to nationally available information, guidance and training provision.

6.3     In responding to requests for advice, an enforcing authority's primary concern should be to provide the advice and guidance necessary to help ensure compliance, and enforcing authorities should consider how they can create an environment in which businesses have confidence in this approach and feel able to seek advice without fear of directly triggering enforcement action.

7.      **An enforcing authority should prioritise the support that it offers to businesses to those that are least likely to have robust compliance arrangements in place, particularly those businesses in priority risk areas[16] (see section 2).**

Guidance:

7.1     Risk assessment should precede and inform all aspects of an enforcing authority's approaches to its regulatory activities[17], including its advice and guidance activities.

7.2     In prioritising the support that it offers, the enforcing authority will want to consider the particular needs of pre-start up and new businesses.

7.3     In prioritising the support that it offers, the enforcing authority will want to consider its responsibilities in respect of businesses based in its area that trade across council boundaries, for example by offering Primary Authority or, where this is not appropriate, acting as a Home Authority.

7.4     Businesses that are in a Primary Authority partnership covering the Age

---

[16] Products, sectors or geographic areas
[17] Regulators' Code, section 3

Restricted Sales category/ies[18] are able to receive authoritative advice in this area from their primary authority. This means that any locally identified need for proactive advice and guidance should be referred to the primary authority.

7.5    Enforcing authorities may find that they can communicate most effectively with local businesses by utilising existing mechanisms, where these exist, for example:

- through trade associations;
- through existing local schemes such as Pubwatch, Business Crime Reduction partnerships, Local Enterprise Partnerships, Purple Flag, Business Improvement Districts, and Community Alcohol Partnerships; and
- through local and trade press.

**8.    An enforcing authority should ensure that the information and guidance that it provides to businesses, their staff, and others, supports a clear and consistent message that valid proof of age must always be required where young people seek to access age restricted products and services through face to face transactions. This information and guidance should be clear in relation to acceptable forms of proof of age.**

Guidance:

8.1    Enforcing authorities will be aware of the risks for young people in relying on a passport or driving licence as proof of age and should consider the advantages of promoting PASS[19] cards as the preferred form of proof of age for businesses and young people in relation to face to face transactions. However, the enforcing authority should acknowledge that there are other acceptable forms of proof of age, as detailed in current Home Office guidance and Gambling Commission guidance.

**9.    A local authority acting as a licensing authority must have regard to the statutory principles of good regulation[20] when considering the attachment of conditions to licences.**

---

[18] The application of Primary Authority to age restricted products is determined by secondary legislation made under the Regulatory Enforcement and Sanctions Act 2008.

[19] The national Proof of Age Standards Scheme, which accredits card issuers to issue proof of age cards bearing the 'PASS hologram'. Information on the Proof of Age Standards Scheme is available at: www.passscheme.org.uk.

[20] The principles set out in section 21 of the Legislative and Regulatory Reform Act 2006, that regulation should be exercised in a way that is transparent, accountable, proportionate and consistent, and is targeted only at cases where it is needed.

Guidance:

9.1     Statutory guidance on the Licensing Act 2003[21] highlights the importance of tailoring licensing conditions to particular premises and ensuring that conditions are appropriate to promote the statutory licensing objectives (ie preventing crime and public nuisance, public safety, and protecting children from harm) and proportionate and do not duplicate other statutory requirements. The guidance rules out standardised conditions which ignore the size, type, location and characteristics and activities taking place at a particular premises, and requires all operational restrictions to be considered and imposed on a case by case basis.

9.2     Statutory guidance on the Gambling Act 2005[22] requires that conditions imposed by the licensing authority should be proportionate to the circumstances which they are seeking to address, and sets out particular factors to be considered in determining proportionate conditions.

9.3     In considering the need for consistency, the licensing authority should not be seeking consistency between all venues in its own area but should ensure that it considers how it can be consistent with advice or guidance that the business has received and relied on in managing its compliance with the licensing objectives.

9.4     Licensing authorities should not impose licensing conditions concerning acceptable forms of proof of age that exclude PASS accredited proof of age cards.

C)      Conduct of checks on compliance

        This Code recognises that checks on compliance in relation to age restricted products and services vary in both their nature and their purpose, and may include inspections of records, processes and procedures, or test purchases. Checks may be undertaken as part of a programme of proactive checks (see 10 below), as part of the response to a local issue (see 11 below), or in response to specific complaints or intelligence about an individual business (see 12 below).

        Targeting: Proactive checks on compliance

---

[21] Amended Guidance Issued Under Section 182 of the Licensing Act 2003, Home Office, 2012, paragraphs 1.16 and 10.10

[22] Guidance to Licensing Authorities, 4th Edition, Gambling Commission 2012

**10.** **Where an enforcing authority chooses to allocate resources to proactive checks on business compliance with legal age restrictions, these should be targeted on the basis of a robust model, scheme or framework for risk assessing the businesses[23].**

Guidance:

10.1   Risk assessment of businesses may be on the basis of a nationally produced risk methodology[24] or on the basis of the enforcing authority's own model. The risk assessment should take account of all relevant, available information and intelligence to make an informed assessment of both the level of hazard, and the likelihood of compliance.

10.2   In relation to the level of hazard consideration should be given to:

- the potential harm associated with the products or services supplied by the business; and
- the number of young people that might access age restricted products and services through the business. For example, consideration should be given to whether the business trades online and, if so, whether it represents a greater risk.

10.3   In relation to the likelihood of compliance[25], ie. the enforcing authority's confidence that the business will manage the hazard appropriately, consideration should be given to the following, where available:

- past compliance records, particularly recent information;
- the existence of systems for managing compliance within the regulated entity;
- evidence of recognised external accreditation, retailer self-testing, or third party tests; and
- management competence and willingness to comply.

10.4   External sources of information and intelligence should be considered where available, for example:

---

[23] Regulators' Code, section 3
[24] For example, the Revised National Trading Standards Board Risk Assessment Scheme, National Trading Standards Board, 2012.
[25] A Common Approach to Risk Assessment, Local Better Regulation Office, 2011

- The secure area of the Primary Authority Register[26] is used by primary authorities to share details of business compliance systems and may be used to publish details of retailer self-testing or the results of national inspection strategies[27] coordinated by the primary authority to seek a picture of compliance across the business's operations.
- The Gambling Commission[28] [29] encourages operators to share the results of third party test purchasing with both themselves and with local authorities. Where such information sharing takes place and the operator can satisfy regulators that they are managing the business risk of underage access themselves this would usually reduce the propensity of the Commission and local authorities to conduct their own compliance checks.
- Operators of schemes[30] that may place relevant requirements on businesses, eg. in relation to age verification policies.

10.5    Where a proactive risk-assessed visit to a business is carried out, the opportunity should be taken to check the operation of the controls that the business has in place to manage its compliance with age restrictions. For example, checks could be carried out on training records or the operation of electronic till prompts.

10.6    Local authorities will need to consider how they will comply with the requirements of the Primary Authority scheme in relation to published inspection plans[31]. Statutory guidance on the scheme[32] requires local authorities to have regard to a published inspection plan when conducting its risk assessment of the business and its programmed activity at the business.

Targeting: Reactive checks on compliance

This part of the Code distinguishes between responding to complaints and information that are not premises-specific (section 11) and complaints or intelligence that relate to a specific business (section 12).

---

[26] The secure area of the Primary Authority Register can be accessed only by registered users. Registration enquiries should be addressed to pa@brdo.bis.gsi.gov.uk.

[27] A primary authority may use an Inspection Plan to put in place a national inspection strategy in relation to a partner business. Guidance on Inspection Plans is available on the Primary Authority Register.

[28] Guidance to Licensing Authorities, 4th Edition, Gambling Commission 2012

[29] Approach to test purchasing – England and Wales only, Gambling Commission, 2011

[30] For example, Best Bar None or the Safer Socialising Award

[31] Primary Authority Handbook, Module 1, Part 3: Inspection Plans, Better Regulation Delivery Office, 2012

[32] Primary Authority Guidance, Local Better Regulation Office, 2009. BRDO is committed to a full review of this statutory guidance in 2013. This review will ensure that the guidance is meeting the needs of local authorities and businesses, and will take into account the development of the Primary Authority scheme since its inception in 2009.

**11.**     **An enforcing authority should ensure that its response to complaints or intelligence about issues in a particular geographic location, or a specific sector, is proportionate.**

Guidance:

11.1     Complaints from local communities often focus on issues in a particular locality eg. drinking in the local park or fireworks being thrown in an area, but information about the source of the age restricted products is not always available. The credibility, quality and quantity of information about potential sources of age restricted products will need to be considered.

11.2     Further information on a local issue may be gathered through community and business engagement, or through the use of observation of the locality[33].

11.3     Businesses may be able to provide the enforcing authority with insight into the nature and extent of any issue, or into any difficulties that they are experiencing, for example, with proxy purchasing, shoplifting, or abusive / threatening behaviour from young people. The enforcing authority may choose to engage with businesses in a locality or sector on an individual basis or through established mechanisms such as through a local Pubwatch scheme or Community Alcohol Partnership.

11.4     When considering its response to such complaints or intelligence the enforcing authority should consider whether the businesses in the locality or sector have been advised of the legal requirements, and may choose to provide or reinforce advice and guidance, as appropriate, or to carry out inspections or other overt checks on the businesses' controls and records[34].

**12.**     **An enforcing authority should ensure that its response to complaints or intelligence about a specific business is proportionate.**

Guidance:

12.1     The credibility, quality and quantity of information about possible breaches of age restricted products and services legislation by a specific business will need to be considered.

---

[32] Section 13 of this Code of Practice refers to statutory requirements for authorisation under the Regulation of Investigatory Powers Act 2000, which should be considered here.

[33] It is unlikely that authorisations under RIPA for covert methods will be considered proportionate without demonstration that overt methods have been attempted and failed.

12.2     In determining whether action is required, and what action might be taken, the enforcing authority should review its knowledge of the business's approach to compliance, its history of compliance, and any mechanism that is available to the enforcing authority to deal with any problems.

12.3     Where the business is in a Primary Authority partnership in relation to Age Restricted Sales, has an active Home Authority relationship, or is regulated by another local or national regulator in respect of age restricted sales, the enforcing authority should consult with that organisation before deciding on the appropriate course of action. For example, where a complaint is received about a business that operates in the gambling sector, the enforcing authority should consult with the Gambling Commission and should establish whether the business has shared compliance data or agreed an action plan with the Gambling Commission.

12.4     Before considering covert test purchasing, the enforcing authority may consider whether it is appropriate to first discuss the complaint(s) or intelligence received with the business.

Test purchasing

This part of the Code addresses the use of test purchasing by young people[35] as a tactic for conducting spot checks on compliance.

**13.       Where an enforcing authority is considering conducting a test purchase exercise, consisting of one or more test purchase attempts, it should consider the statutory requirements for authorisation under the Regulation of Investigatory Powers Act 2000, as amended. It is unlikely that authorisations under RIPA for covert methods will be considered proportionate without demonstration that overt methods have been attempted and failed.**

Guidance:

13.1     Authorisation is required for 'directed surveillance' and the use of 'covert human intelligence sources' (CHIS). Guidance published by the Office of Surveillance Commisioners includes the following:

'When a young person, pursuant to an arrangement with an officer of a public authority, carries out a test purchase at a shop, he is unlikely

---

[35] In the context of this code, 'young people' includes any child, young person or young adult.

to be construed as a CHIS on a single transaction but this would change if the juvenile revisits the same establishment in a way that encourages familiarity. If covert recording equipment is worn by the test purchaser, or an adult is observing the test purchase, it will be desirable to obtain an authorisation for directed surveillance because the ECHR has construed the manner in which a business is run as private information and such authorisation must identify the premises involved. In all cases a prior risk assessment is essential in relation to a young person.'

'When conducting covert test purchase operations at more than one establishment, it is not necessary to construct an authorisation for each premise to be visited but the intelligence must be sufficient to prevent 'fishing trips'. Premises may be combined within a single authorisation provided that each is identified at the outset. Necessity, proportionality and collateral intrusion must be carefully addressed in relation to each of the premises. It is unlikely that authorisations will be considered proportionate without demonstration that overt methods have been attempted and failed.'

Decisions to deviate from the guidance will have to be justified to the Office of Surveillance Commisioners.

13.2   There are specific provisions in relation to working with covert human intelligence sources who are under eighteen in the Regulation of Investigatory Powers (Juveniles) Order 2000, which enforcing authorities should be aware of.

13.3   Statutory codes of practice in relation to authorisations for directed surveillance[36] and the use of CHIS[37] are produced by the Home Office and are available on its website, along with guidance[38] on the recent changes to the authorisation requirements implemented under the Protection of Freedoms Act 2012.

13.4   A request for authorisation of test purchasing would usually set out the tactics to be used, the reasons for using these tactics, and the factors considered in determining their necessity and proportionality. In considering necessity and proportionality, the following pointers may be useful:

---

[36] Covert Surveillance and Property Interference Revised Code of Practice, Home Office, 2010
[37] Covert Human Intelligence Sources Code of Practice, Home Office, 2010
[38] Protection of Freedoms Act 2012 – changes to provisions under the Regulation of Investigatory Powers Act 2000. Home Office Guidance to local authorities in England and Wales on the judicial approval process for RIPA and the crime threshold for directed surveillance, Home Office, 2012

- Is there evidence that the business will only sell to young people that it recognises, that means that repeated test purchasing by the same young person is envisaged?
- Does the context in which the test purchase will take place mean that the test purchaser might be endangered by answering questions about his or her age honestly?
- Has the business failed to follow previous advice eg. by continuing to ask a prospective purchaser his or her age, rather than asking for valid proof of age?

14.   **Where a decision is made, in accordance with the preceding provisions of this Code, to conduct a test purchase exercise:**

a)   **A test purchaser should be selected, with regard to:**
   - **his or her age and appearance (see Section 23);**
   - **his or her suitability for the type of premises to be visited eg. 'on' licence or 'off' licence premises;**
   - **his or her suitability for the tactics to be deployed, understanding that his or her welfare[39] is paramount; and**
   - **the likelihood that he or she will be recognised in the locations to be visited (eg. proximity to their home or school).**

b)   **The test purchaser may be allowed or instructed to dress as a young person normally would for visiting the particular type of establishment where the test purchase(s) are to be attempted, and to wear such jewellery and make-up as he or she would normally wear for visiting that type of establishment[40].**

c)   **The test purchaser may be allowed or instructed to present proof of age if they are asked for this by the business being tested. This proof of age should be genuine and should relate to the test purchaser. Where there are concerns about revealing the identity of the test purchaser, the proof of age should not include any identifying details such as name or address.**

d)   **The test purchaser should be instructed on any particular tactics to be used; should understand the reasons for using the tactics and how they may be used; and his or her consent to use such tactics should be obtained.**

e)   **Enforcing authorities will need to be aware that the use of a test purchaser aged under 18 should be authorised by the appropriate person in relation**

---

[39] See section 19 of this Code.

[40] Note that statutory defence provisions in section 146 of the Licensing Act 2003 make reference to an individual's appearance: '....nobody could reasonably have suspected from the individual's appearance that he was aged under 18....' Enforcing authorities will need to have regard to these provisions in determining whether the appearance of a test purchaser is suitable.

to test purchases under the Licensing Act 2003[41] or the Gambling Act 2005[42].

15.     Where an enforcing authority conducts a test purchase attempt in relation to compliance with age restricted products and services legislation, whether or not in response to a complaint or other intelligence, the business should be notified in writing of the outcome of the test purchase attempt. Written notifications of test purchases should include the following:

a) The fact that a test took place, and an indication of the time period within which the test took place. (This does not require disclosure of the exact time or date though the enforcing authority may feel that it is helpful to provide this detail where they do not have specific concerns about the welfare of the test purchaser.)

b) Any reason for the test eg. as part of a survey, or in response to complaints about sales of age restricted products by businesses in the area or the particular business.

c) The premises address.

d) The category of product and relevant legislation.

e) The outcome of the test.

f) Where relevant, a note that there was a failure to request valid proof of age[43].

g) The name of the seller, where known.

Guidance:

15.1    The publication of generic details of exercises eg. locality, number of premises visited, failure rate, product, age of volunteers etc. by the enforcing authority may be of value but is not a replacement for individual notification.

15.2    Template letters that enforcing authorities may choose to use will be made available on BRDO's website.

16.     Written notifications pursuant to section 15 above should be sent to the following person(s):

---

[41] A young person under 18 years who buys or attempts to buy alcohol may commit an offence (Licensing Act 2003, section 149(1)) unless this is at the request of 'a constable or a weights and measures inspector who is acting in the course of his duties' (section 149(2)).

[42] A young person under 18 years who gambles may commit an offence (Gambling Act 2005) unless this is 'at the request of a constable, enforcement officer or authorised person acting in the performance of his functions' (section 64).

[43] Where the enforcing authority feels that advice on improving compliance is needed, they should refer this to the primary authority where relevant.

a)  To the owner of the business, whether identified from the Companies Act 2006 notice displayed on the premises, or otherwise.

b)  In the case of alcohol, to the Premises Licence Holder, with a copy also being sent to the legal owner of the alcohol, if a different person.

Guidance:

16.1   The code does not require written notifications to be sent to employees or members of staff, unless there is a particular reason to notify them.

16.2   Where the business is in a Primary Authority partnership in relation to Age Restricted Products or Age Restricted Services, regard should be had to any recommendations or advice of the Primary Authority in respect of communication, for example in an inspection plan in relation to age restricted sales.

17.   **Where a test purchaser accesses the age restricted product or service ('failed test'), written notifications should be made promptly after the test purchase has taken place, and should be seen as supplementary to any verbal notification that may be given at the time of the test purchase.**

Guidance:

17.1   A timescale of up to 5 working days would be considered to be 'prompt' for the purposes of this section.

17.2   An enforcing authority might consider delaying notification under this section in specific circumstances, for example, where the enforcing authority has credible evidence of deliberate disregard of the law and foresees that it is likely to consider enforcement action. In this circumstance, it might be reasonable for the enforcing authority to delay written notification beyond 5 working days, whilst it carries out further test purchases in a short space of time, in order to gather further evidence.

17.3   It would not usually be appropriate for the enforcing authority to delay notification under this section in order to protect the identity of the test purchaser or officers involved in the test purchase operation, unless further test purchases are planned at the premises using those same individuals, within a short space of time (as outlined above).

17.4   Any decision to delay notification should be taken on a case by case basis and the reasons for the decision should be recorded.

18.     **Where a test purchaser is denied access to the age restricted product or service ('passed test'), written notifications should be made within a reasonable period of time.**

Guidance:

18.1    A timescale of up to 10 working days would be considered to be 'reasonable' for the purposes of this section.

18.2    An enforcing authority might consider delaying notification under this section in specific circumstances. For example:

- where there are valid concerns about identification of the test purchaser or accompanying officers by a particular business; or
- where the enforcing authority has credible evidence of continuing disregard of the law and wishes to follow up the test purchase with further test purchases in a short space of time.

18.3    It would not usually be appropriate for the enforcing authority to delay notification under this section in respect of a business that has demonstrated a responsible approach to compliance, for example through working within a Primary Authority partnership that covers age restricted sales compliance.

18.4    Any decision to delay notification should be taken on a case by case basis and the reasons for the decision should be recorded.

**Welfare of young people**

19.     **An enforcing authority that recruits and engages young people as test purchasers must ensure that, in the conduct of its operations, the welfare of children is always paramount[44]. In particular the enforcing authority should:**

a)  **Consider the need to protect the identity of each test purchaser at all times.**
b)  **Carry out a risk assessment[45] in respect of each test purchasing operation, in accordance with the health and safety procedures of the enforcing authority.**

---

[44] Statutory guidance issued under s.16 of the Children Act 2004 and s.7 of the Local Authorities Social Services Act 1970 underlines the need to ensure that the welfare of children is paramount in the discharge of all local authority functions.
[45] The term 'risk assessment' is used throughout this Code to refer to the assessment of the risk posed by a business. However, in this section of the Code it is used to refer to an assessment of the risks that an enforcement activity presents to the health and safety of participants in the activity.

c) Consider whether officers undertaking work with young persons should complete a disclosure in accordance with the enforcing authority's policy[46].

d) Design working arrangements with a view to optimising protection for the test purchaser.

In particular, it is recommended that:

- officers visit young people under the age of 18 (test purchasers or prospective test purchasers) only in the presence of a parent, guardian, teacher or other responsible adult;
- arrangements for engaging a young person under the age of 18 for a test purchase operation are always made with a parent or guardian;
- a test purchaser under the age of 18 should always be collected from and returned by officers to a place of safety that has been agreed in advance with a parent or guardian, and a parent, guardian, teacher or other responsible adult should usually be present when the test purchaser is collected and returned, unless it has been agreed in advance that this is not necessary;
- consideration is given to whether an officer should be present in the premises during the test purchase attempt and, where this is not possible or appropriate, what other arrangements may be made to allow the test purchaser to easily contact an officer;
- consideration is given to whether one of the officers accompanying the young person should be of the same gender as the young person;
- consideration should be given to conducting test purchase attempts in such a way as to minimise the likelihood that the test purchaser will be called to give evidence; and that
- an exercise or operation should be halted if at any point a young person shows signs of distress or indicates a reluctance to continue.

Guidance:

19.1    To facilitate the protection of a test purchaser's identity, the enforcing authority may find it helpful to assign a unique identity code to each test purchaser. This code can then be used to refer to the test purchaser in all documentation associated with a test purchase. The enforcing authority may then consider marking records which link this code to the identity of the test purchaser as sensitive material.

---

[46] Guidance on criminal record checks is available on the Disclosure and Barring Service website at: https://www.gov.uk/government/organisations/disclosure-and-barring-service

19.2   A template health and safety risk assessment that may be used by enforcing authorities will be made available on BRDO's website.

**20.   Young people may be 'recruited' to participate in test purchase operations from any appropriate source. An explanation should be provided to the young people at the recruitment stage of the purpose and nature of test purchase operations, and the possible outcomes where an illegal sale is made.**

Guidance:

20.1   Appropriate sources for recruitment of test purchasers may include:

- through work with local schools, colleagues or youth groups;
- from relatives of staff of the enforcing authority or partner organisations;
- from existing employees of the enforcing authority or its partners; or
- volunteer police cadets.

**21.   Where the enforcing authority employs young people as test purchasers it will need to have particular regard to the statutory requirements[47] [48] in respect of employing workers of the relevant age.**

**22.   The provision of any form of payment, reward or gratuity to a test purchaser should not include any element that is dependent upon the outcome of the test purchase.**

**23.   Where a young person expresses an interest in assisting the enforcing authority, consideration should be given to his or her suitability for participation in test purchase exercises.**

Guidance:

23.1   An assessment of suitability should give consideration to the following factors:

- How old is the young person? To be considered suitable for test purchase operations that aim to establish whether illegal sales are being made, the young person should be younger than the legal age limit for the product that is to be test purchased.

---

[47] Working Time Regulations 1998; Children and Young Persons Act 1933 (employment of 'children', and local authority powers to make byelaws relating to the employment of children); Education Act 1996 (defines 'child' and 'compulsory school age'); Education and Skills Act 2008
[48] Guidance on the Employment of Children, Department for Education, 2009

- Does the young person's appearance fairly reflect their age? To be considered suitable for test purchase operations that aim to establish whether illegal sales are being made, the young person's appearance should lead a reasonable person to suspect that they are below the legal age limit for the product to be test purchased[49].
- What appears to be motivating the prospective test purchaser to participate? A young person who apears to be overly keen to 'catch out' a business should not be considered suitable as a test purchaser.

24.   **Where a young person is assessed as suitable, a comprehensive explanation should be provided to him or her as a prospective test purchaser of the matters listed below and his or her written agreement should be obtained. Where the prospective test purchaser is below 18 this explanation should also be given to his or her parent or guardian and the agreement of his or her parent or guardian to the young person's participation should be obtained.**

a)   **The purpose of test purchase operations.**
b)   **The practical arrangements for conduct of operations.**
c)   **The arrangements that are in place to ensure the welfare of test purchasers.**
d)   **The conditions attached to participation eg. whether the test purchaser will receive payment or reward of any kind.**
e)   **The possible outcomes where an illegal sale is made.**

Guidance:

24.1   A template test purchaser agreement form that may be used by enforcing authorities will be made available on BRDO's website.

25.   **Evidence of the date of birth of the young person should be seen by an officer of the enforcing authority, prior to recruiting a young person as a test purchaser.**

Guidance:

25.1   Acceptable evidence of the prospective test purchaser's date of birth might include:

---

[49] Note that the statutory defence provisions in section 146 of the Licensing Act 2003 make reference to an individual's appearance: '...nobody could reasonably have suspected from the individual's appearance that he was aged under 18...' Enforcing authorities will need to have regard to these provisions in determining whether the appearance of a test purchaser is suitable.

- the young person's photo card driving licence;
- the young person's passport;
- a PASS accredited proof of age card; or
- a copy of the young person's birth certificate, endorsed by the young person's parent or carer.

25.2    In most circumstances, the officer will want to keep a copy of the proof of identity seen.

**26.    Prior to each exercise or operation, the test purchaser's consent to participation should be obtained and, where the test purchaser is below 18, consent to his or her participation in the exercise or operation should also be obtained from his or her parent or guardian.**

Guidance:

26.1    The tactics that have been authorised for an exercise or operation should be explained to the young person and the potential implications for the young person should be clear to him or her before consent is sought from the young person and his or her parent or guardian. In particular, the young person should understand that, if a situation arises where he or she is called to give evidence in Court, he or she may be questioned in relation to the use of the particular tactics.

26.2    The enforcing authority should determine its requirements for consent. For example, it may choose to require written consent or to accept verbal consent as long as this is recorded by an officer.

**27.    Prior to each exercise or operation in which they have agreed to participate, test purchasers should be given detailed instructions, appropriate to the nature of the exercise and the type of establishment to be visited.**

Guidance:

27.1    The enforcing authority may find it helpful to provide the test purchaser with written instructions as to how they should conduct the proposed test purchases, and to obtain a signature on these instructions as an indication of understanding.

27.2    Instructions would normally include:

- to dress as a young person normally would for visiting the particular type of establishment where the test purchase(s) are to be attempted, and to wear such jewellery and make-up as he or she would normally wear for visiting that type of establishment[50];

- the practical arrangements for his or her welfare during the exercise or operation;
- not to volunteer information about his or her age or identity to the seller;
- not to enter into conversation with the seller where a sale is refused or to make any attempt to persuade the seller to make a sale;
- to leave the premises immediately if he or she feels uncomfortable with the situation that he or she is in;
- how to respond where the seller asks any questions about his or her age; and
- how to respond if he or she is asked to produce his or her proof of age.

D) Responses to non-compliance

**28.     The enforcing authority should ensure that it communicates effectively with the business in relation to any non-compliance, and with any individual who may be responsible for the non-compliance.**

Guidance:

28.1     The enforcing authority will need to ensure that it communicates with the most appropriate person within the business. Where the business has a primary authority or home authority, early contact with it will usually be helpful in identifying the most effective route of communication, whether this is to obtain information from the business, or to ensure that compliance issues are addressed promptly.

28.2     Statutory guidance on the Licensing Act 2003[51] identifies it as good practice for responsible authorities to give licence holders 'early warning of their concerns about 'problems identified at the premises concerned and of the need for improvement'. This would involve discussions with a representative of the business who has the authority to address issues. Where the business is a multi-site operator, discussions at premises level, for example with the designated premises supervisor or other staff, may be needed but would not replace discussions with the licence holder.

---

[50] Note that the statutory defence provisions in section 146 of the Licensing Act 2003 make reference to an individual's appearance: '…nobody could reasonable have suspected from the individual's appearance that he was aged under 18…' Enforcing authorities will need to have regard to these provisions in determining whether the appearance of a test purchaser is suitable.

[51] Amended Guidance Issued under Section 182 of the Licensing Act 2003, Home Office, 2012, paragraph 11.10

28.3    In responding to a non-compliance, an enforcing authority's primary focus will usually be on securing future compliance. In most circumstances, this requires constructive dialogue with the business in order for both parties to understand the causes of the non-compliance and any changes that are needed. It is recognised that, where the enforcing authority is at the same time considering enforcement action and is investigating a potential criminal offence, the requirements of the investigation may inhibit this constructive dialogue. The enforcing authority will need to consider how it manages this dual role to best deliver its regulatory outcomes.

28.4    Where an investigation is initiated, the enforcing authority should ensure that the business is aware of the investigation and knows when it can expect updates on the progress of the investigation. The outcome of the investigation should be notified promptly to the business, whether that is a decision to take no further action, a warning letter, the initiation of enforcement action, or some other outcome.

28.5    The enforcing authority should ensure that it is transparent about any future implications of enforcement action that it takes. In particular, it should be clear to the business how accepting a simple caution or receiving a warning notice might influence future enforcement action. For example, where the enforcing authority might use the simple caution or warning notice as evidence of persistent selling.

**29.    The enforcing authority should ensure that it responds to non-compliance in a manner that complies with that authority's published policy[52] and with the principles set out in the Macrory Review[53], namely, that their approach should:**

- **aim to change the behaviour of the offender and to secure ongoing compliance;**
- **aim to eliminate any financial gain or benefit from non-compliance;**
- **be responsive and consider what is appropriate for the particular offender and regulatory issue, which can include punishment and the public stigma that should be associated with a criminal conviction;**
- **be proportionate to the nature of the offence and the harm caused; and**
- **aim to restore the harm caused by regulatory non-compliance, where appropriate.**

---

[52] Regulators' Code, section 6
[53] Regulatory Justice: Making Sanctions Effective, Better Regulation Executive, 2006

Guidance:

29.1   In considering a response to non-compliance that is proportionate, the enforcing authority will wish to consider all factors that it has identified as causing or contributing to the breach, and will want to make an assessment as to the business's attitude to compliance. This will help it to decide whether it can work with the business to support the achievement of ongoing compliance (see 29.2 below), or whether it is appropriate to deal firmly with the business (see 29.3 below).

29.2   An enforcing authority's approach to supporting the business to achieve ongoing compliance might include:
   • providing advice or guidance to the business;
   • working in partnership to address issues identified in local implementation of a business's controls at a particular premises;
   • accepting a commitment from the business to take specified steps to secure ongoing compliance (agreeing an 'action plan'); and
   • agreeing a course of remedial action with a primary authority or home authority for the business, or with the Premises Licence Holder, where appropriate.

29.3   An enforcing authority should take firm enforcement action where it is needed, having regard to the public interest, the available evidence and the circumstances of each case. For example, factors to consider may include the following:

   • Where there is evidence of criminal activity for which there is a reasonable prospect of conviction and it would be in the public interest to proceed with enforcement action, for example, because the regulatory issue in question is one which represents a particularly high priority.
   • Where there is evidence of persistent selling[54] [55].
   • Where there is evidence of failure to demonstrate due diligence or taking reasonable steps to establish the age of the individual.
   • Where the non-compliance involved aggravating factors. Eg. 'hide it up your sleeve'; 'I can't sell it to you now but come round the back later'; 'just wait until other customers have left the shop'. The Government's Tobacco Control Plan 'Healthy Lives, Healthy People' sets out the Government's view that: '... enforcement action should only be needed in cases where the law

---

[54] Licensing Act 2003, section 147A
[55] Children and Young Persons Act 1933, sections 12A to 12D

is deliberately flouted, but where it happens, we support local authorities in taking strong action'[56].

- Where advice and/ or support to the business has not been effective in improving compliance.

29.4   The enforcing authority should consider how it will ensure that its responses to non-compliance are proportionate where responsibility for the non-compliance rests with an employee or employees, or other individual(s) who work in the business.

29.5   Licensing authorities are required to act in accordance with the statutory principles of good regulation[57] and are required to have regard to the statutory guidance issued under section 182 of the Licensing Act 2003 and section 25 of the Gambling Act 2005.

11.5   Regulation of Investigatory Powers

The Protection of Freedoms Act 2012 has precipitated a change of emphasis on the applicability of the Regulation of Investigatory Powers Act 2000 (RIPA) to test purchase operations by local authorities. There has, over the years of the existence of RIPA been a gradual tightening of the guidance around when officers are deploying directed surveillance or covert human intelligence sources. The most recent government guidance was published in December 2014[57].

Firstly a local authority has to consider whether or not its test purchasing activity is directed surveillance. To be directed surveillance, all of the following must be true:

- It is covert, but not intrusive surveillance :
- It is conducted for the purposes of a specific investigation or operation;
- It is likely to result in the obtaining of private information about a person (whether or not one specifically identified for the purposes of the investigation or operation);
- It is conducted otherwise than by way of an immediate response to events or circumstances the nature of which is such that it would not be reasonably practicable for an authorisation under Part II of RIPA to be sought.

---

[56] Note that the Tobacco Control Action Plan for Wales does not include this statement.

[57] The principles set out in section 21 of the Legislative and Regulatory Reform Act 2006, that regulation should be exercised in a way that is transparent, accountable, proportionate and consistent, and is targeted only at cases where it is needed.

Under age test purchasing may be considered to be part of the general observation duties of a local authority, but the specific guidance includes an example as follows:

> "Intelligence suggests that a local shopkeeper is openly selling alcohol to underage customers, without any questions being asked. A trained employee or person engaged by a public authority is deployed to act as a juvenile in order to make a purchase of alcohol. In these circumstances any relationship, if established at all, is likely to be so limited in regards to the requirements of that Act, that a public authority may conclude that a covert human intelligence source (CHIS) authorisation is unnecessary. However, if the test purchaser is wearing recording equipment and is not authorised as a CHIS, or an adult is observing, consideration should be given to granting a directed surveillance authorisation."

Although there is no case law yet available on this, it seems likely that local authorities will consider it more likely than not that a RIPA authorisation would be required for their standard test purchasing tactics and almost definitely required if they are engaged in any particular tactics like building up a relationship with the seller, lying about age or using other false pretences.

However, it would seem that pre-screening (that is sending an young person over the age of 18 in to attempt a purchase) where that young person is unaccompanied by an observer but merely walks into a premises, lawfully purchases an age restricted product but observes whether or not they are challenged for ID in accordance with any stated age verification policy would not be likely to require authorisation as either a CHIS or for directed surveillance.

The key addition to the most recent guidance is the addition of the words 'or an adult is observing' to the example shown above. Previously, the guidance only suggested directed surveillance authorisation was required if the young person was wearing recording equipment. This recognised the greater risks of collateral intrusion[58] where body-worn surveillance equipment is used. However, the newer guidance would cover the more common scenario where an evidence gathering officer is inside the premises witnessing the sale taking place in order to give evidence of same without calling the young person to give evidence of the sale. In these circumstances and in accordance with the new guidance, it would seem more likely than not that directed surveillance

---

[58] Regulation of Investigatory Powers (Directed Surveillance and Covert Human Intelligence Sources) (Amendment) Order 2012 (SI 2012:1500)

authority would be required for the more usual test purchasing tactics.

On 1 November 2012, the Protection of Freedoms Act 2012 made significant changes to the availability of RIPA to local authorities (but not the Police). By s.37 of the 2012 Act, a local authority authorisation under RIPA for either directed surveillance or a covert human intelligence source, must be approved by a Magistrate. In addition, the crime threshold for when local authorities can use RIPA authorisations was significantly increased.

Firstly, an officer of the rank of Director, Head of Service or Service Manager has to go through the RIPA Office authorisation process. The Interception of Communications Commissioner's Office has indicated that a Principal Trading Standards Officer is not considered to be of sufficient seniority to act as the Designated Person for RIPA Authorisations.

Local Authorities can only authorise directed surveillance related to offences where punishment on conviction has a maximum term of at least 6 months imprisonment or relates to an underage sale of alcohol, tobacco or a nicotine inhaling product[59]. In relation to under age sales, therefore, that would only relate to:

- Alcohol
- Tobacco or tobacco products
- Nicotine inhaling products
- Knives or bladed instruments (.s,141A(1) Criminal Justice Act 1988 (penalty six months imprisonment))
- Crossbows (s.1 Crossbows Act 1987 (penalty six months imprisonment))
- Firearms (s.22(1) Firearms Act 1968 (penalty six months imprisonment))
- Gambling (s.46 – 47 Gambling Act 2005 (penalty six months imprisonment))
- National Lottery (s.13(1) National Lottery Act 1993 (penalty two years imprisonment))
- Fireworks (s.12(1) Consumer Protection Act 1987 (penalty six months imprisonment))
- Solvents/Intoxicating Substances (s.1(1) Intoxicating Substances (Supply) Act 1985 (penalty six months imprisonment)
- Cigarette Lighter Refills (s.12(1) Consumer Protection Act 1987 (penalty six months imprisonment))
- Petrol (Health and Safety at Work etc Act 1974 (penalty six months imprisonment))

---

[59] See R.7A(3)(b) of the Regulation of Investigatory Powers (Directed Surveillance and Covert Human Intelligence Sources) (Amendment) Order 2010 (SI2010:521) as amended in 2012 (SI 2012:1500)

- Video Recordings/Games (s. 11(1) Video Recordings Act 1984 (penalty six months imprisonment))
- Cinemas (s.136(1) Licensing Act 2003 (penalty six months imprisonment))
- Sex Establishment (para 23, sch 3 Local Government (Miscellaneous Provisions) Act 1982 (penalty six months imprisonment))
- Body Piercing of Genitalia or sexual parts (penalty 14 years imprisonment))
- Pet animals (s.11 Animal Welfare Act 2006 (penalty 51 weeks imprisonment))
- Clinical Trials (Medicines for Human Use (Clinical Trials) Regulations 2004 (penalty two years imprisonment))
- Tooth Whitening Products (Cosmetic Products Enforcement Regulations 2013 (Penalty one year imprisonment))

However, there would be no availability to conduct test purchasing by a local authority under a directed surveillance authority for any of the following as they fall below the crime threshold. Any test purchasing for these activities will require Police RIPA authorisation:

- Harmful Publications
- Tattoos
- Hypnotism
- Sunbeds

It should also be noted that it is an offence for a person under 18 to attempt to purchase firearms and crossbows, so evidence of under age sales would need to be founded on evidence obtained other than by test purchasing.

## 11.6    Principles of Better Regulation

By section 21 of the Legislative and Regulatory Reform Act 2006, local authorities[60] exercising powers related to the vast majority of age restricted sales legislation must have regard to the Principles of Better Regulation. These are that:

- Regulatory activities should be carried out in a way which is transparent, accountable, proportionate and consistent
- Regulatory activities should be targeted only at cases in which action is needed

On 6th April 2014, a statutory code of practice came into force and regulators must have regard to the code when determining policies, setting standards or giving guidance in relation to their duties.

---

[60] Legislative and Regulatory Reform (Regulatory Functions) Order 2007 (SI2007:3544)

The original 2008 code was drafted in response to the Hampton Review[61] of the UK's regulatory system, which proposed the principles of better regulation based on a risk-based approach and proportionality to regulatory enforcement.

## 11.7    Regulators Code

Regulators whose functions are specified by order under section 24(2) of the Legislative and Regulatory Reform Act 2006 must have regard to the Code when developing policies and operational procedures that guide their regulatory activities. Regulators must equally have regard to the Code when setting standards or giving guidance which will guide the regulatory activities of other regulators. If a regulator concludes, on the basis of material evidence, that a specific provision of the Code is either not applicable or is outweighed by another relevant consideration, the regulator is not bound to follow that provision, but should record that decision and the reasons for it.

**1.      Regulators should carry out their activities in a way that supports those they regulate to comply and grow**

1.1      Regulators should avoid imposing unnecessary regulatory burdens through their regulatory activities and should assess whether similar social, environmental and economic outcomes could be achieved by less burdensome means. Regulators should choose proportionate approaches to those they regulate, based on relevant factors including, for example, business size and capacity.

1.2      When designing and reviewing policies, operational procedures and practices, regulators should consider how they might support or enable economic growth for compliant businesses and other regulated entities, for example, by considering how they can best:

- understand and minimise negative economic impacts of their regulatory activities;
- minimising the costs of compliance for those they regulate;
- improve confidence in compliance for those they regulate, by providing greater certainty; and
- encourage and promote compliance.

1.3      Regulators should ensure that their officers have the necessary knowledge and

---

[61] HM Treasury: Reducing Administrative Burdens – Effective Inspections and Enforcement (2005) a report by Philip Hampton

skills to support those they regulate, including having an understanding of those they regulate that enables them to choose proportionate and effective approaches.

1.4     Regulators should ensure that their officers understand the statutory principles of good regulation and of this Code, and how the regulator delivers its activities in accordance with them.

**2.     Regulators should provide simple and straightforward ways to engage with those they regulate and hear their views**

2.1     Regulators should have mechanisms in place to engage those they regulate, citizens and others to offer views and contribute to the development of their policies and service standards. Before changing policies, practices or service standards, regulators should consider the impact on business and engage with business representatives.

2.2     In responding to non-compliance that they identify, regulators should clearly explain what the non-compliant item or activity is, the advice being given, actions required or decisions taken, and the reasons for these. Regulators should provide an opportunity for dialogue in relation to the advice, requirements or decisions, with a view to ensuring that they are acting in a way that is proportionate and consistent.

        This paragraph does not apply where the regulator can demonstrate that immediate enforcement action is required to prevent or respond to a serious breach or where providing such an opportunity would be likely to defeat the purpose of the proposed enforcement action.

2.3     Regulators should provide an impartial and clearly explained route to appeal against a regulatory decision or a failure to act in accordance with this Code. Individual officers of the regulator who took the decision or action against which the appeal is being made should not be involved in considering the appeal. This route to appeal should be publicised to those who are regulated.

2.4     Regulators should provide a timely explanation in writing of any right to representation or right to appeal. This explanation should be in plain language and include practical information on the process involved.

2.5     Regulators should make available to those they regulate, clearly explained complaints procedures, allowing them to easily make a complaint about the conduct of the regulator.

2.6     Regulators should have a range of mechanisms to enable and regularly invite, receive and take on board customer feedback, including, for example, through customer satisfaction surveys of those they regulate.

**3.      Regulators should base their regulatory activities on risk**

3.1     Regulators should take an evidence based approach to determining the priority risks in their area of responsibility, and should allocate resources where they would be most effective in addressing those priority risks.

3.2     Regulators should consider risk at every stage of their decision-making processes, including choosing the most appropriate type of intervention or way of working with those regulated; targeting checks on compliance; and when taking enforcement action.

3.3     Regulators designing a risk assessment framework, for their own use or for use by others, should have mechanisms in place to consult on the design with those affected, and to review it regularly.

3.4     Regulators, in making their assessment of risk, should recognise the compliance record of those they regulate, including using earned recognition approaches and should consider all available and relevant data on compliance, including evidence of relevant external verification.

3.5     Regulators should review the effectiveness of their chosen regulatory activities in delivering the desired outcomes and make any necessary adjustments accordingly.

**4.      Regulators should share information about compliance and risk**

4.1     Regulators should collectively follow the principle of "collect once, use many times" when requesting information from those they regulate.

4.2     When the law allows, regulators should agree secure mechanisms to share information with each other about businesses and other bodies they regulate, to help target resources and activities and minimise duplication.

**5.      Regulators should ensure clear information, guidance and advice is available to help those they regulate meet their responsibilities to comply**

5.1     Regulators should provide advice and guidance that is focused on assisting those they regulate to understand and meet their responsibilities. When providing advice and guidance, legal requirements should be distinguished from suggested good practice and the impact of the advice or guidance should be considered so that it does not impose unnecessary burdens in itself.

5.2     Regulators should publish guidance, and information in a clear, accessible, concise format, using media appropriate to the target audience and written in plain language for the audience.

5.3     Regulators should have mechanisms in place to consult those they regulate in relation to the guidance they produce to ensure that it meets their needs.

5.4     Regulators should seek to create an environment in which those they regulate have confidence in the advice they receive and feel able to seek advice without fear of triggering enforcement action.

5.5     In responding to requests for advice, a regulator's primary concerns should be to provide the advice necessary to support compliance, and to ensure that the advice can be relied on.

5.6     Regulators should have mechanisms to work collaboratively to assist those regulated by more than one regulator. Regulators should consider advice provided by other regulators and, where there is disagreement about the advice provided, this should be discussed with the other regulator to reach agreement.

**6.      Regulators should ensure that their approach to their regulatory activities is transparent**

6.1     Regulators should publish a set of clear service standards, setting out what those they regulate should expect from them.

6.2     Regulators' published service standards should include clear information on:

a)  how they communicate with those they regulate and how they can be contacted;
b)  their approach to providing information, guidance and advice;
c)  their approach to checks on compliance, including details of the risk assessment framework used to target those checks as well as protocols for their conduct, clearly setting out what those they regulate should expect;
d)  their enforcement policy, explaining how they respond to non-compliance;
e)  their fees and charges, if any. This information should clearly explain the basis on which these are calculated, and should include an explanation of whether compliance will affect fees and charges; and

f)  how to comment or complain about the service provided and routes to appeal.

6.3   Information published to meet the provisions of this Code should be easily accessible, including being available at a single point on the regulator's website that is clearly signposted, and it should be kept up to date.

6.4   Regulators should have mechanisms in place to ensure that their officers act in accordance with their published service standards, including their enforcement policy.

6.5   Regulators should publish, on a regular basis, details of their performance against their service standards, including feedback received from those they regulate, such as customer satisfaction surveys, and data relating to complaints about them and appeals against their decisions.

# TABLE OF RESTRICTED GOODS

This table shows a list of products or services that have mandatory age restrictions applied to them.

| Description of Goods/Service | Age for Purchase | Legislation | Any Particular Circumstances Required |
|---|---|---|---|
| Acetone (nail polish remover) | 18 | Intoxicating Substances (Supply) Act 1985 | If seller has reasonable grounds to believe the substance will be used by that person to cause intoxication. |
| Adult gaming centre | 18 | Gambling Act 2005 | |
| Aerosols (other than spray paint) | 18 | Intoxicating Substances (Supply) Act 1985 | If seller has reasonable grounds to believe the substance will be used by that person to cause intoxication. |
| Air cartridges (for airguns) | 18 | Firearms Act 1968 | |
| Air weapons | 18 | Firearms Act 1968 | |
| Alcohol | 18 | Licensing Act 2003 | |
| Alcopops | 18 | Licensing Act 2003 | |
| Allergy reliefs (containing diphenhydramine or dimenhydrinate) | 18 | Intoxicating Substances (Supply) Act 1985 | If seller has reasonable grounds to believe the substance will be used by that person to cause intoxication. |

| Description of Goods/Service | Age for Purchase | Legislation | Any Particular Circumstances Required |
|---|---|---|---|
| Ammunition | 18 | Firearms Act 1968 | |
| Anal piercing | 16 | Sexual Offences Act 2003 | |
| Animal liniments | 18 | Intoxicating Substances (Supply) Act 1985 | If seller has reasonable grounds to believe the substance will be used by that person to cause intoxication. |
| Animals | 16 | Animal Welfare Act 2006 | |
| Anti-freeze | 18 | Intoxicating Substances (Supply) Act 1985 | If seller has reasonable grounds to believe the substance will be used by that person to cause intoxication. |
| Arbitrage betting | 18 | Gambling Act 2005 | |
| Arrows (for crossbows) | 18 | Crossbows Act 1987 | |
| Assault rifles | 18 | Firearms Act 1968 | |
| Athame knives | 18 | Criminal Justice Act 1988 | |
| Balisongs | 18 | Criminal Justice Act 1988 | These bladed instruments may only be sold if they are antiques (over 100 years old) and then may not be sold to persons under 18 years. |
| Ball bearing (BB) guns | 18 | Firearms Act 1968 | |
| Ballistic knives | 18 | Firearms Act 1968 | |

| Description of Goods/Service | Age for Purchase | Legislation | Any Particular Circumstances Required |
|---|---|---|---|
| Barbeque lighting sticks (containing butane) | 18 | Cigarette Lighter Refills (Safety) Regulations 1999 | |
| Bayonets | 18 | Criminal Justice Act 1988 | |
| Beer | 18 | Licensing Act 2003 | Can be consumed by those aged 16 or 17 in licensed premises with an adult whilst eating a table meal. |
| Belt buckle knives | 18 | Criminal Justice Act 1988 | These bladed instruments may only be sold if they are antiques (over 100 years old) and then may not be sold to persons under 18 years. |
| Betting | 18 | Gambling Act 2005 | |
| Bingo | 18 | Gambling Act 2005 | |
| Birds | 16 | Animal Welfare Act 2006 | |
| Blu-ray Discs | 12/15/18 | Video Recordings Act 1984 | |
| Boning knives | 18 | Criminal Justice Act 1988 | |
| Bows (parts for a crossbow) | 18 | Crossbows Act 1987 | |
| Brandy | 18 | Licensing Act 2003 | |
| Bread knives | 18 | Criminal Justice Act 1988 | |

| Description of Goods/Service | Age for Purchase | Legislation | Any Particular Circumstances Required |
|---|---|---|---|
| Breast piercing (girls) | 16 | Sexual Offences Act 2003 | |
| Bullets | 18 | Firearms Act 1968 | |
| Butane | 18 | Cigarette Lighter Refills (Safety) Regulations 1999 | |
| Butcher's knives | 18 | Criminal Justice Act 1988 | |
| Butterfly Knives | 18 | Criminal Justice Act 1988 | These bladed instruments may only be sold if they are antiques (over 100 years old) and then may not be sold to persons under 18 years. |
| Camping gas stove refills | 18 | Cigarette Lighter Refills (Safety) Regulations 1999 Must contain butane. | |
| Carbines | 18 | Firearms Act 1968 | |
| Carving knives | 18 | Criminal Justice Act 1988 | |
| Cartridges (ammunition) | 18 | Firearms Act 1968 | |
| Casinos | 18 | Gambling Act 2005 | |
| Cats | 16 | Animal Welfare Act 2006 | |
| Chef's knives | 18 | Criminal Justice Act 1988 | |
| Chew plugs | 18 | Children and Young Persons Act 1933 | Niche tobacco product |
| Chimó | 18 | Children and Young Persons Act 1933 | Niche tobacco product |
| Christmas crackers | 12 | Pyrotechnic Articles (Safety) Regulations 2010 | |

| Description of Goods/Service | Age for Purchase | Legislation | Any Particular Circumstances Required |
|---|---|---|---|
| Cider | 18 | Licensing Act 2003 | Can be consumed by those aged 16 or 17 in licensed premises with an adult whilst eating a table meal. |
| Cigarette lighter refills | 18 | Cigarette Lighter Refills (Safety) Regulations 1999 | Must contain butane. |
| Cigarettes | 18 | Children and Young Persons Act 1933 | |
| Cigars | 18 | Children and Young Persons Act 1933 | |
| Cinema films | 12/15/18 | Licensing Act 2003 | |
| Cleavers | 18 | Criminal Justice Act 1988 | |
| Clinical trials | 16 | Medicines for Human Use (Clinical Trials) Regulations 2004 | |
| CO2 airguns | 18 | Firearms Act 1968 | |
| Cocktails | 18 | Licensing Act 2003 | Must have an alcoholic strength (when served) of greater than 0.5% by volume. |
| Combat knives | 18 | Criminal Justice Act 1988 | |
| Comics (containing harmful images) | 18 | Children and Young Persons (Harmful Publications) Act 1955 | |
| Correcting fluid | 18 | Intoxicating Substances (Supply) Act 1985 | If seller has reasonable grounds to believe the substance will be used by that person to cause intoxication. |

| Description of Goods/Service | Age for Purchase | Legislation | Any Particular Circumstances Required |
|---|---|---|---|
| Cough suppressants (containing dextromethorphan) | 18 | Intoxicating Substances (Supply) Act 1985 | If seller has reasonable grounds to believe the substance will be used by that person to cause intoxication. |
| Cracker snaps | 16 | Pyrotechnic Articles (Safety) Regulations 2010 | |
| Creamy snuff | 18 | Children and Young Persons Act 1933 | Niche tobacco product |
| Credit | 18 | Consumer Credit Act 1974 | |
| Crossbows | 18 | Crossbows Act 1987 | |
| Cyanoacrylate (super glue) | 18 | Intoxicating Substances (Supply) Act 1985 | If seller has reasonable grounds to believe the substance will be used by that person to cause intoxication. |
| Cyclohexyl nitrite (commonly called poppers) | 18 | Intoxicating Substances (Supply) Act 1985 | If seller has reasonable grounds to believe the substance will be used by that person to cause intoxication. |
| Daggers | 18 | Criminal Justice Act 1988 | |
| Dextromethorphan (a cough suppressant) – known as DXM | 18 | Intoxicating Substances (Supply) Act 1985 | If seller has reasonable grounds to believe the substance will be used by that person to cause intoxication. |
| Digital versatile discs (DVDs) | 12/15/18 | Video Recordings Act 1984 | |

| Description of Goods/Service | Age for Purchase | Legislation | Any Particular Circumstances Required |
|---|---|---|---|
| Dog racing tracks | 18 | Gambling Act 2005 | Only applies to restricted areas as per the race track licence. |
| Dogs | 16 | Animal Welfare Act 2006 | |
| Diver's knives | 18 | Criminal Justice Act 1988 | |
| Dry cleaning fluid | 18 | Intoxicating Substances (Supply) Act 1985 | If seller has reasonable grounds to believe the substance will be used by that person to cause intoxication. |
| Electric knives | 18 | Criminal Justice Act 1988 | |
| Family entertainment centres | 18 | Gambling Act 2005 | Only applies to the sections of a family entertainment centre that contains category C gaming machines |
| Fantasy sports leagues | 18 | Gambling Act 2005 If they require payment of an entry fee and have prizes. | |
| Filter tips (for tobacco) | 18 | Children and Young Persons Act 1933 | |
| Firearms | 18 | Firearms Act 1968 | |
| Fireworks (category 2,3,4) | 18 | Pyrotechnic Articles (Safety) Regulations 2010 | |
| Fish (alive) | 16 | Animal Welfare Act 2006 | |
| Fixed odds betting | 18 | Gambling Act 2005 | |
| Folding pocket knives | 18 | Criminal Justice Act 1988 | Must have either a locking blade or a blade in excess of 3 inches (7.62cm) |

| Description of Goods/Service | Age for Purchase | Legislation | Any Particular Circumstances Required |
|---|---|---|---|
| Football pools | 16 | Gambling Act 2005 | |
| Footclaws | 18 | Criminal Justice Act 1988 | These bladed instruments may only be sold if they are antiques (over 100 years old) and then may not be sold to persons under 18 years. |
| Fuse wire containing gunpowder | 16 | Explosives Act 1875 | |
| Gambling | 18 | Gambling Act 2005 | |
| Gaming machines (categories A,B & C) | 18 | Gambling Act 2005 | |
| Gas cartridges (for airguns) | 18 | Firearms Act 1968 | |
| Gas ram airguns | 18 | Firearms Act 1968 | |
| Gentleman's clubs (licensed sexual entertainment venue) | 18 | Local Government (Miscellaneous Provisions) Act 1982 | |
| Gin | 18 | Licensing Act 2003 | |
| Grenades | 18 | Firearms Act 1968 | |
| Gul | 18 | Children and Young Persons Act 1933 | Niche tobacco product |
| Gunpowder | 16 | Explosives Act 1875 | |
| Gutkha | 18 | Children and Young Persons Act 1933 | Niche tobacco product |

| Description of Goods/Service | Age for Purchase | Legislation | Any Particular Circumstances Required |
|---|---|---|---|
| Handclaws | 18 | Criminal Justice Act 1988 | These bladed instruments may only be sold if they are antiques (over 100 years old) and then may not be sold to persons under 18 years. |
| Handguns | 18 | Firearms Act 1968 | |
| Harmful publications | 18 | Children and Young Persons (Harmful Publications) Act 1955 | |
| Hollow kubotan | 18 | Criminal Justice Act 1988 | These bladed instruments may only be sold if they are antiques (over 100 years old) and then may not be sold to persons under 18 years. |
| Horse liniments | 18 | Intoxicating Substances (Supply) Act 1985 | If seller has reasonable grounds to believe the substance will be used by that person to cause intoxication. |
| Horse racing tracks | 18 | Gambling Act 2005 | Only applies to restricted areas as per the race track licence. |
| Horses | 16 | Animal Welfare Act 2006 | |
| Hypnotism | 18 | Hypnotism Act 1952 | Must be at or in connection with an entertainment to which the public are admitted, whether on payment or otherwise. |
| Imitation firearms | 18 | Violent Crime Reduction Act 2006 | May only be sold in limited circumstances to persons over 18 years. |

| Description of Goods/Service | Age for Purchase | Legislation | Any Particular Circumstances Required |
|---|---|---|---|
| Incense products containing synthetic cannabinoids | 18 | Intoxicating Substances (Supply) Act 1985 | If seller has reasonable grounds to believe the substance will be used by that person to cause intoxication. |
| Indoor fireworks (category 1) | 16 | Pyrotechnic Articles (Safety) Regulations 2010 | |
| Iq'mik | 18 | Children and Young Persons Act 1933 | Niche tobacco product |
| Jimson weed (datura stramonium) | 18 | Intoxicating Substances (Supply) Act 1985 | If seller has reasonable grounds to believe the substance will be used by that person to cause intoxication. |
| Keno (gambling) | 18 | Gambling Act 2005 | |
| Khaini | 18 | Children and Young Persons Act 1933 | Niche Tobacco Product |
| Kilayas (Buddhist ceremonial knives) | 18 | Criminal Justice Act 1988 | |
| Kirpans (Sikh ceremonial swords) | 18 | Criminal Justice Act 1988 | |
| Knives | 18 | Criminal Justice Act 1988 | |
| Kris daggers | 18 | Criminal Justice Act 1988 | |
| Kusari gama | 18 | Criminal Justice Act 1988 | These bladed instruments may only be sold if they are antiques (over 100 years old) and then may not be sold to persons under 18 years. |

| Description of Goods/Service | Age for Purchase | Legislation | Any Particular Circumstances Required |
|---|---|---|---|
| Kyoketsu shoge | 18 | Criminal Justice Act 1988 | These bladed instruments may only be sold if they are antiques (over 100 years old) and then may not be sold to persons under 18 years. |
| Lager | 18 | Licensing Act 2003 | Can be consumed by those aged 16 or 17 in licensed premises with an adult whilst eating a table meal. |
| Lap dancing | 18 | Local Government (Miscellaneous Provisions) Act 1982 | |
| Leather cleaners | 18 | Intoxicating Substances (Supply) Act 1985 | If seller has reasonable grounds to believe the substance will be used by that person to cause intoxication. |
| Letter openers | 18 | Criminal Justice Act 1988 | |
| Linoleum knives | 18 | Criminal Justice Act 1988 | |
| Liqueurs | 18 | Licensing Act 2003 | |
| Loans | 18 | Consumer Credit Act 1974 | |
| Loose leaf chew | 18 | Children and Young Persons Act 1933 | Niche tobacco product |
| Lotteries | 16 | Gambling Act 2005 | See also 'National Lottery' |
| Machetes | 18 | Criminal Justice Act 1988 | |

| Description of Goods/Service | Age for Purchase | Legislation | Any Particular Circumstances Required |
|---|---|---|---|
| Machine guns | 18 | Firearms Act 1968 | |
| Magazines (if they contain a video work) | 12/15/18 | Video Recordings Act 1984 | |
| Manrikigusari | 18 | Criminal Justice Act 1988 | These bladed instruments may only be sold if they are antiques (over 100 years old) and then may not be sold to persons under 18 years. |
| Marker pens | 18 | Intoxicating Substances (Supply) Act 1985 | If seller has reasonable grounds to believe the substance will be used by that person to cause intoxication. |
| Mawa | 18 | Children and Young Persons Act 1933 | Niche Tobacco Product |
| Methoxetamine (MXE) known as 'Mexxy' | 18 | Intoxicating Substances (Supply) Act 1985 | If seller has reasonable grounds to believe the substance will be used by that person to cause intoxication. MXE has been temporarily prohibited from import or sale in the UK pending a decision on whether or not it should be added to the Schedules in the Misuse of Drugs Act 1971. |
| Mishri (Masheri, Misheri) | 18 | Children and Young Persons Act 1933 | Niche tobacco product |
| Moist plug | 18 | Children and Young Persons Act 1933 | Niche tobacco product |

| Description of Goods/Service | Age for Purchase | Legislation | Any Particular Circumstances Required |
|---|---|---|---|
| Multitools | 18 | Criminal Justice Act 1988 | |
| Muskets | 18 | Firearms Act 1968 | |
| Nail polish remover | 18 | Intoxicating Substances (Supply) Act 1985 | If seller has reasonable grounds to believe the substance will be used by that person to cause intoxication. |
| Nass | 18 | Children and Young Persons Act 1933 | Niche Tobacco Product |
| National lottery | 16 | National Lottery Act 1993 | |
| Newspapers (if they contain a video work) | 12/15/18 | Video Recordings Act 1984 | |
| Nicotine lozenges | 18 | Children and Young Persons Act 1933 | Niche tobacco product |
| Nipple piercing (girls) | 16 | Sexual Offences Act 2003 | |
| Nitrous oxide (laughing gas) | 18 | Intoxicating Substances (Supply) Act 1985 | If seller has reasonable grounds to believe the substance will be used by that person to cause intoxication. |
| Novelty matches | 16 | Pyrotechnic Articles (Safety) Regulations 2010 | |
| Nutmeg spices | 18 | Intoxicating Substances (Supply) Act 1985 | If seller has reasonable grounds to believe the substance will be used by that person to cause intoxication. |
| Odorisers | 18 | Intoxicating Substances (Supply) Act 1985 | If seller has reasonable grounds to believe the substance will be used by that person to cause intoxication. |

| Description of Goods/Service | Age for Purchase | Legislation | Any Particular Circumstances Required |
|---|---|---|---|
| On Demand Programme Services | 18 | Communications Act 2003 | Applies to R18 or R18-equivallent material |
| Oven cleaners | 18 | Intoxicating Substances (Supply) Act 1985 | If seller has reasonable grounds to believe the substance will be used by that person to cause intoxication. |
| Oyster knives | 18 | Criminal Justice Act 1988 | |
| Pachinko (gambling) | 18 | Gambling Act 2005 | |
| Pain relief sprays | 18 | Intoxicating Substances (Supply) Act 1985 | If seller has reasonable grounds to believe the substance will be used by that person to cause intoxication. |
| Paint strippers | 18 | Intoxicating Substances (Supply) Act 1985 | If seller has reasonable grounds to believe the substance will be used by that person to cause intoxication. |
| Paraffin | 16 | | |
| Party poppers | 16 | Pyrotechnic Articles (Safety) Regulations 2010 | |
| Pan masala (betel quid) | 18 | Children and Young Persons Act 1933 | Niche tobacco product |
| Papers (for tobacco) | 18 | Children and Young Persons Act 1933 | |
| Parimutuel betting | 18 | Gambling Act 2005 | |
| Pellets (for airguns or firearms) | 18 | Firearms Act 1968 | |
| Penis piercing | 16 | Sexual Offences Act 2003 | |

| Description of Goods/Service | Age for Purchase | Legislation | Any Particular Circumstances Required |
|---|---|---|---|
| Percussion caps (not intended for toys) | 16 | Pyrotechnic Articles (Safety) Regulations 2010 | |
| Petrol | 16 | Petroleum (Consolidation) Regulations 2014 | |
| Pets | 16 | Animal Welfare Act 2006 | |
| Piercing (breasts, nipples, vagina, penis, anus) | 16 | Sexual Offences Act 2003 | |
| Pistols | 18 | Firearms Act 1968 | |
| Plugs (chew) | 18 | Children and Young Persons Act 1933 | Niche tobacco product |
| Pneumatic airguns (PCP) | 18 | Firearms Act 1968 | |
| Polyvinyl acetate (PVA) glues | 18 | Intoxicating Substances (Supply) Act 1985 | If seller has reasonable grounds to believe the substance will be used by that person to cause intoxication. |
| Poppers (nitrites) | 18 | Intoxicating Substances (Supply) Act 1985 | If seller has reasonable grounds to believe the substance will be used by that person to cause intoxication. |
| Poppy seeds or pods | 18 | Intoxicating Substances (Supply) Act 1985 | If seller has reasonable grounds to believe the substance will be used by that person to cause intoxication. |
| Pools (football) | 16 | Gambling Act 2005 | |
| Projectiles (for ammunition) | 18 | Firearms Act 1968 | |

| Description of Goods/Service | Age for Purchase | Legislation | Any Particular Circumstances Required |
|---|---|---|---|
| Puukko woodcraft knives | 18 | Criminal Justice Act 1988 | |
| Push dagger | 18 | Criminal Justice Act 1988 | These bladed instruments may only be sold if they are antiques (over 100 years old) and then may not be sold to persons under 18 years. |
| Pyrotechnics | 18 | Pyrotechnic Articles (Safety) Regulations 2010 | Some pyrotechnics are restricted to sale for professional use only. |
| Qiwam (Kimam) | 18 | Children and Young Persons Act 1933 | Niche Tobacco Product |
| Race tracks | 18 | Gambling Act 2005 | Only applies to restricted areas as per the race track licence. |
| Raffles | 16 | Gambling Act 2005 | Certain small and non-commercial raffles are exempt |
| Rampuri (Indian fighting knife) | 18 | Criminal Justice Act 1988 | |
| Razor blades | 18 | Criminal Justice Act 1988 | Exempt if less than 2mm of the blade is showing. |
| Replica firearms | 18 | Violent Crime Reduction Act 2006 | May only be sold in limited circumstances to persons over 18 years. |
| Reptiles | 16 | Animal Welfare Act 2006 | |
| Rifles | 18 | Firearms Act 1968 | |
| Rolling tobacco | 18 | Children and Young Persons Act 1933 | |

| Description of Goods/Service | Age for Purchase | Legislation | Any Particular Circumstances Required |
|---|---|---|---|
| Rum | 18 | Licensing Act 2003 | |
| Saws | 18 | Criminal Justice Act 1988 | Except certain types of blunt pointed saws like pruning saws or plasterboard saws. |
| Scalpels | 18 | Criminal Justice Act 1988 | |
| Scrap metal | 16 | Scrap Metal Dealers Act 1964 | |
| Scratchcards (National Lottery) | 16 | National Lottery Act 1993 | |
| Scratchcards (non-National Lottery) | 16 | Gambling Act 2005 | |
| Seax knives | 18 | Criminal Justice Act 1988 | |
| Serpents | 16 | Pyrotechnic Articles (Safety) Regulations 2010 | |
| Sex cinemas (licensed) | 18 | Local Government (Miscellaneous Provisions) Act 1982 | |
| Sexual entertainment centres (licensed) | 18 | Local Government (Miscellaneous Provisions) Act 1982 | |
| Sex shops (licensed) | 18 | Local Government (Miscellaneous Provisions) Act 1982 | |
| Sgian Dubh (a type of dagger worn with highland dress (kilts)) | 18 | Criminal Justice Act 1988 | |

| Description of Goods/Service | Age for Purchase | Legislation | Any Particular Circumstances Required |
|---|---|---|---|
| Shandy | 18 | Licensing Act 2003 | Must have an alcoholic strength (when served) of greater than 0.5% by volume. |
| Sherry | 18 | Licensing Act 2003 | |
| Shot (for shotguns) | 18 | Firearms Act 1968 | |
| Shotguns | 18 | Firearms Act 1968 | |
| Shuriken | 18 | Criminal Justice Act 1988 | These bladed instruments may only be sold if they are antiques (over 100 years old) and then may not be sold to persons under 18 years. |
| Sleeping aids (containing diphenhydramine or dimenhydrinate) | 18 | Intoxicating Substances (Supply) Act 1985 | If seller has reasonable grounds to believe the substance will be used by that person to cause intoxication. |
| Slot machines | 18 | Gambling Act 2005 | Certain low stake, low prize machines are not age restricted (category D) |
| Snuff | 18 | Children and Young Persons Act 1933 | Niche tobacco product |
| Snus (Snuff) | 18 | Children and Young Persons Act 1933 | Niche tobacco product |
| Solvents | 18 | Intoxicating Substances (Supply) Act 1985 | If seller has reasonable grounds to believe the substance will be used by that person to cause intoxication. |
| Sparklers | 18 | Pyrotechnic Articles (Safety) Regulations 2010 | |

| Description of Goods/Service | Age for Purchase | Legislation | Any Particular Circumstances Required |
|---|---|---|---|
| Spirits (alcohol) | 18 | Licensing Act 2003 | |
| Spray paint | 16 | Anti-Social Behaviour Act 2003 | |
| Spread betting | 18 | Gambling Act 2005 | |
| Spring-piston airguns | 18 | Firearms Act 1968 | |
| Sunbeds (use of in a business premises) | 18 | Sunbeds (Regulation) Act 2010 | |
| Sunbeds (use of in a domestic premises) | 18 | Sunbeds (Regulation) Act 2010 | Only applies in Wales |
| Sunbeds (for purchase or hire to take away) | 18 | Sunbeds (Regulation) Act 2010 | Only applies in Wales |
| Stage pyrotechnics | 18 | Pyrotechnic Articles (Safety) Regulations 2010 | Some pyrotechnics are restricted to sale for professional use only. |
| Super glue | 18 | Intoxicating Substances (Supply) Act 1985 | If seller has reasonable grounds to believe the substance will be used by that person to cause intoxication. |
| Swordsticks | 18 | Criminal Justice Act 1988 | These bladed instruments may only be sold if they are antiques (over 100 years old) and then may not be sold to persons under 18 years. |
| Tanning salons (restricted zones) | 18 | Sunbeds (Regulation) Act 2010 | |

| Description of Goods/Service | Age for Purchase | Legislation | Any Particular Circumstances Required |
|---|---|---|---|
| Tape head cleaning fluid | 18 | Intoxicating Substances (Supply) Act 1985 | If seller has reasonable grounds to believe the substance will be used by that person to cause intoxication. |
| Tattoos | 18 | Tattooing of Minors Act 1969 | |
| Teeth Whitening Products | 18 | Cosmetic Products Enforcement Regulations 2013 | |
| Throw downs | 16 | Pyrotechnic Articles (Safety) Regulations 2010 | |
| Tobacco | 18 | Children & Young Persons Act 1933 | |
| Toluene marker pens | 18 | Intoxicating Substances (Supply) Act 1985 | If seller has reasonable grounds to believe the substance will be used by that person to cause intoxication. |
| Toombak | 18 | Children and Young Persons Act 1933 | Niche tobacco product |
| Tooth powder | 18 | Children and Young Persons Act 1933 | Niche tobacco product |
| Trench knives | 18 | Criminal Justice Act 1988 | |
| Twist roll (chew) | 18 | Children and Young Persons Act 1933 | Niche tobacco product |
| Unrealistic imitation firearms | 18 | Violent Crime Reduction Act 2006 | |
| Vaginal piercing | 16 | Sexual Offences Act 2003 | |
| Video games | 12/16/18 | Video Recordings Act 1984 | PEGI Ratings are now also mandatory. |

| Description of Goods/Service | Age for Purchase | Legislation | Any Particular Circumstances Required |
|---|---|---|---|
| Video poker | 18 | Gambling Act 2005 | |
| Vodka | 18 | Licensing Act 2003 | |
| Waterpipe tobacco smoking | 18 | Children and Young Persons Act 1933 | Niche tobacco product |
| White spirit | 16 | Petroleum (Consolidation) Act 1928 | Only applicable at a licensed petrol filling station |
| Wine | 18 | Licensing Act 2003 | Can be consumed by those aged 16 or 17 in licensed premises with an adult whilst eating a table meal. |
| X-acto knives | 18 | Criminal Justice Act 1988 | |
| Xylene marker pens | 18 | Intoxicating Substances (Supply) Act 1985 | If seller has reasonable grounds to believe the substance will be used by that person to cause intoxication. |
| Zarda | 18 | Children and Young Persons Act 1933 | Niche Tobacco Product |

## EXTRACTS OF STATUTES

### Animal Welfare Act 2006

11 Transfer of animals by way of sale or prize to persons under 16.

(1)     A person commits an offence if he sells an animal to a person whom he has reasonable cause to believe to be under the age of 16 years.

(2)     For the purposes of subsection (1), selling an animal includes transferring, or agreeing to transfer, ownership of the animal in consideration of entry by the transferee into another transaction.

(3)     Subject to subsections (4) to (6), a person commits an offence if—
(a)he enters into an arrangement with a person whom he has reasonable cause to believe to be under the age of 16 years, and
(b)the arrangement is one under which that person has the chance to win an animal as a prize.

(4)     A person does not commit an offence under subsection (3) if—
(a)he enters into the arrangement in the presence of the person with whom the arrangement is made, and
(b)he has reasonable cause to believe that the person with whom the arrangement is made is accompanied by a person who is not under the age of 16 years.

(5)     A person does not commit an offence under subsection (3) if—
(a)he enters into the arrangement otherwise than in the presence of the person with whom the arrangement is made, and
(b)he has reasonable cause to believe that a person who has actual care and control of the person with whom the arrangement is made has consented to the arrangement.

(6)     A person does not commit an offence under subsection (3) if he enters into the arrangement in a family context

### Anti-social behaviour Act 2003

### 54      Sale of aerosol paint to children

(1)     A person commits an offence if he sells an aerosol paint container to a person under the age of sixteen.

(2)     In subsection (1) "aerosol paint container" means a device which—
(a) contains paint stored under pressure, and
(b) is designed to permit the release of the paint as a spray.

(3)     A person guilty of an offence under this section shall be liable on summary

conviction to a fine not exceeding level 4 on the standard scale.

(4)      It is a defence for a person charged with an offence under this section in respect of a sale to prove that—

(a) he took all reasonable steps to determine the purchaser's age, and

(b) he reasonably believed that the purchaser was not under the age of sixteen.

(5)      It is a defence for a person charged with an offence under this section in respect of a sale effected by another person to prove that he (the defendant) took all reasonable steps to avoid the commission of an offence under this section.

**Children and Young Persons Act 1933**

5 Giving intoxicating liquor to children under five

If any person gives, or causes to be given, to any child under the age of five years any alcohol (within the meaning given by section 191 of the Licensing Act 2003, but disregarding subsection (1)(f) to (i) of that section), except upon the order of a duly qualified medical practitioner, or in case of sickness, apprehended sickness, or other urgent cause, he shall, on summary conviction, be liable to a fine not exceeding level 1 on the standard scale.

7 Sale of tobacco, &c. to persons under eighteen

(1)      Any person who sells to a person under the age of eighteen years any tobacco or cigarette papers, whether for his own use or not, shall be liable, on summary conviction to a fine not exceeding level 4 on the standard scale.

(1A)     It shall be a defence for a person charged with an offence under subsection (1) above to prove that he took all reasonable precautions and exercised all due diligence to avoid the commission of the offence.

(2)      If on complaint to a magistrates' court it is proved to the satisfaction of the court that any automatic machine for the sale of tobacco kept on any premises has been used by any person under the age of eighteen years, the court shall order the owner of the machine, or the person on whose premises the machine is kept, to take such precautions to prevent the machine being so used as may be specified in the order or, if necessary, to remove the machine, within such time as may be specified in the order, and if any person against whom such an order has been made fails to comply therewith, he shall be liable, on summary conviction, to a fine not exceeding level 4 on the standard scale.

(3)      It shall be the duty of a constable and of a park-keeper being in uniform to seize any tobacco or cigarette papers in the possession of any person apparently under the age of sixteen years whom he finds smoking in any street or public place, and any tobacco or cigarette papers so seized shall be disposed of, if seized by a constable, in such manner as the police authority may direct, and if

seized by a park-keeper, in such manner as the authority or person by whom he was appointed may direct.

(4)     Nothing in this section shall make it an offence to sell tobacco or cigarette papers to, or shall authorise the seizure of tobacco or cigarette papers in the possession of, any person who is at the time employed by a manufacturer of or dealer in tobacco, either wholesale or retail, for the purposes of his business, or is a boy messenger in uniform in the employment of a messenger company and employed as such at the time.

(5)     For the purposes of this section the expression "tobacco" includes cigarettes any product containing tobacco and intended for oral or nasal use and smoking mixtures intended as a substitute for tobacco, and the expression "cigarettes" includes cut tobacco rolled up in paper, tobacco leaf, or other material in such form as to be capable of immediate use for smoking.

12A Restricted premises orders.

(1)     This section applies where a person ("the offender") is convicted of a tobacco offence ("the relevant offence").

(2)     The person who brought the proceedings for the relevant offence may by complaint to a magistrates' court apply for a restricted premises order to be made in respect of the premises in relation to which that offence was committed ("the relevant premises").

(3)     A restricted premises order is an order prohibiting the sale on the premises to which it relates of any tobacco or cigarette papers to any person.

(4)     The prohibition applies to sales whether made—
(a)by the offender or any other person, or
(b)by means of any machine kept on the premises or any other means.

(5)     The order has effect for the period specified in the order, but that period may not exceed one year.

(6)     The applicant must, after making reasonable enquiries, give notice of the application to every person appearing to the applicant to be a person affected by it.

(7)     The court may make the order if (and only if) it is satisfied that—
(a)on at least 2 occasions within the period of 2 years ending with the date on which the relevant offence was committed, the offender has committed other tobacco offences in relation to the relevant premises, and
(b)the applicant has complied with subsection (6).

(8)     Persons affected by the application may make representations to the court as to why the order should not be made.

(9)     If—
(a)a person affected by an application for a restricted premises order was not given notice under subsection (6), and
(b)consequently the person had no opportunity to make representations to the

court as to why the order should not be made, the person may by complaint apply to the court for an order varying or discharging it.

(10)     On an application under subsection (9) the court may, after hearing—
(a)that person, and
(b)the applicant for the restricted premises order, make such order varying or discharging the restricted premises order as it considers appropriate.

(11)     For the purposes of this section the persons affected by an application for a restricted premises order in respect of any premises are—
(a)the occupier of the premises, and
(b)any other person who has an interest in the premises.

12B Restricted sale orders.

(1)     This section applies where a person ("the offender") is convicted of a tobacco offence ("the relevant offence").

(2     )The person who brought the proceedings for the relevant offence may by complaint to a magistrates' court apply for a restricted sale order to be made in respect of the offender.

(3)     A restricted sale order is an order prohibiting the person to whom it relates—
(a)from selling any tobacco or cigarette papers to any person,
(b)from having any management functions in respect of any premises in so far as those functions relate to the sale on the premises of tobacco or cigarette papers to any person,
(c)from keeping any cigarette machine on any premises for the purpose of selling tobacco or permitting any cigarette machine to be kept on any premises by any other person for that purpose, and
(d)from having any management functions in respect of any premises in so far as those functions relate to any cigarette machine kept on the premises for the purpose of selling tobacco.

(4)     The order has effect for the period specified in the order, but that period may not exceed one year.

(5)     The court may make the order if (and only if) it is satisfied that, on at least 2 occasions within the period of 2 years ending with the date on which the relevant offence was committed, the offender has committed other tobacco offences.

(6)     In this section any reference to a cigarette machine is a reference to an automatic machine for the sale of tobacco.

12C Enforcement.

(1)     If—
(a) a person sells on any premises any tobacco or cigarette papers in contravention of a restricted premises order, and

(b) the person knew, or ought reasonably to have known, that the sale was in contravention of the order, the person commits an offence.

(2)     If a person fails to comply with a restricted sale order, the person commits an offence.

(3)     It is a defence for a person charged with an offence under subsection (2) to prove that the person took all reasonable precautions and exercised all due diligence to avoid the commission of the offence.

(4)     A person guilty of an offence under this section is liable, on summary conviction, to a fine not exceeding £20,000.

(5     A restricted premises order is a local land charge and in respect of that charge the applicant for the order is the originating authority for the purposes of the Local Land Charges Act 1975.

12D Interpretation.

(1)     In sections 12A and 12B a "tobacco offence" means—
(a)an offence committed under section 7(1) on any premises (which are accordingly "the premises in relation to which the offence is committed"),
(b)an offence committed under section 7(2) in respect of an order relating to any machine kept on any premises (which are accordingly "the premises in relation to which the offence is committed"), or
(c)an offence committed under section 3A of the Children and Young Persons (Protection from Tobacco) Act 1991 in respect of any machine kept on any premises (which are accordingly "the premises in relation to which the offence is committed").

(2)     In sections 12A to 12C the expressions "tobacco" and "cigarette" have the same meaning as in section 7.

(3)     In sections 12A and 12B "notice" means notice in writing.

## Children and Young Persons (Harmful Publications) Act 1955

1       Works to which this Act applies

This Act applies to any book, magazine or other like work which is of a kind likely to fall into the hands of children or young persons and consists wholly or mainly of stories told in pictures (with or without the addition of written matter), being stories portraying—
(a)the commission of crimes; or
(b)acts of violence or cruelty; or
(c)incidents of a repulsive or horrible nature;
in such a way that the work as a whole would tend to corrupt a child or young person into whose hands it might fall.

2        Penalty for printing, publishing, selling, &c., works to which this Act applies

(1)      A person who prints, publishes, sells or lets on hire a work to which this Act applies, or has any such work in his possession for the purpose of selling it or letting it on hire, shall be guilty of an offence and liable, on summary conviction, to imprisonment for a term not exceeding four months or to a fine not exceeding level 3 on the standard scale or to both:

Provided that, in any proceedings taken under this subsection against a person in respect of selling or letting on hire a work or of having it in his possession for the purpose of selling it or letting it on hire, it shall be a defence for him to prove that he had not examined the contents of the work and had no reasonable cause to suspect that it was one to which this Act applies.

(2)      A prosecution for an offence under this section shall not, in England or Wales, be instituted except by, or with the consent of, the Attorney General.

5        Short title, interpretation, extent, commencement and duration

(1)      This Act may be cited as the Children and Young Persons (Harmful Publications) Act 1955.

(2)      In this Act the expressions "child" and "young person" have the meanings assigned to them respectively by section one hundred and seven of the Children and Young Persons Act 1933,... the expression "plate" (except where it occurs in the expression "photographic plate") includes block, mould, matrix and stencil and the expression "photographic film" includes photographic plate.


**Cigarette Lighter Refill (Safety) Regulations 1999**

2        No person shall supply any cigarette lighter refill canister containing butane or a substance with butane as a constituent part to any person under the age of eighteen years.

**Consumer Credit Act 1974**

50 Circulars to minors.

(1)      A person commits an offence, who, with a view to financial gain, sends to a minor any document inviting him to—
         (a)borrow money, or
         (b)obtain goods on credit or hire, or

(c)obtain services on credit, or

(d)apply for information or advice on borrowing money or otherwise obtaining credit, or hiring goods.

(2)    In proceedings under subsection (1) in respect of the sending of a document to a minor, it is a defence for the person charged to prove that he did not know, and had no reasonable cause to suspect, that he was a minor.

(3)    Where a document is received by a minor at any school or other educational establishment for minors, a person sending it to him at that establishment knowing or suspecting it to be such an establishment shall be taken to have reasonable cause to suspect that he is a minor.

**Criminal Justice Act 1988**

**S.141A[1] Sale of knives and certain articles with a blade or point to persons under eighteen[2]**

(1)    Any person who sells to a person under the age of eighteen years an article to which this section applies shall be guilty of an offence and liable on summary conviction to imprisonment for a term not exceeding six months, or a fine not exceeding level 5 of the standard scale, or both.

(2)    Subject to subsection (3) below, this section applies to –

(a)    any knife, knife blade or razor blade,

(b)    any axe,

(c)    any other article which has a blade or which is sharply pointed and which is made or adapted for use for causing injury to the person.

(3)    This section does not apply to any article described in –

(a)    section 1 of the Restriction of Offensive Weapons Act 1959 (c.37),

(b)    an order made under section 141(2) of this Act[3], or

(c)    an order made by the Secretary of State under this section[4].

(4)    It shall be a defence for a person charged with an offence under subsection (1) above to prove that he took all reasonable precautions and exercised all due diligence to avoid the commission of the offence.

---

[1] S.141A inserted by s. 6(1)(3) of the Offensive Weapons Act 1996 (c.26) and brought into force by SI 1996/3063 on 01/01/1997)

[2] Inserted by ss. 43(2), 66(2) of the Violent Crime Reduction Act 2006 (c.38) and brought into force by SI 2007/2180, art.3(j) on 01/10/2007)

[3] The Criminal Justice Act 1988 (Offensive Weapons) Order 1988, SI 1988/1668 has been made.

[4] The Criminal Justice Act 1988 (Offensive Weapons) (Exemptions) Order 1996, SI 1996/3064 has been made.

**Crossbows Act 1987**

**1  Sale and letting on hire.**

A person who sells or lets on hire a crossbow or a part of a crossbow to a person under the age of eighteen is guilty of an offence, unless he believes him to be seventeen years of age or older and has reasonable ground for the belief.

**2  Purchase and hiring.**

A person under the age of eighteen who buys or hires a crossbow or a part of a crossbow is guilty of an offence.

**3  Possession.**

A person under the age of eighteen who has with him
(a) a crossbow which is capable of discharging a missile, or
(b) parts of a crossbow which together (and without any other parts) can be assembled to form a crossbow capable of discharging a missile, is guilty of an offence, unless he is under the supervision of a person who is twenty-one years of age or older.

**4  Powers of search and seizure etc.**

(1)  If a constable suspects with reasonable cause that a person is committing or has committed an offence under section 3, the constable may
(a) search that person for a crossbow or part of a crossbow;
(b) search any vehicle, or anything in or on a vehicle, in or on which the constable suspects with reasonable cause there is a crossbow, or part of a crossbow, connected with the offence.
(2)  A constable may detain a person or vehicle for the purpose of a search under subsection (1).
(3)  A constable may seize and retain for the purpose of proceedings for an offence under this Act anything discovered by him in the course of a search under subsection (1) which appears to him to be a crossbow or part of a crossbow.
(4)  For the purpose of exercising the powers conferred by this section a constable may enter any land other than a dwelling-house.

**5  Exception.**

This Act does not apply to crossbows with a draw weight of less than 1.4 kilograms.

**6**       **Punishments.**

(1)       A person guilty of an offence under section 1 shall be liable, on summary conviction, to imprisonment for a term not exceeding six months, to a fine not exceeding level 5 on the standard scale, or to both.

(2)       A person guilty of an offence under section 2 or 3 shall be liable, on summary conviction, to a fine not exceeding level 3 on the standard scale.

(3)       The court by which a person is convicted of an offence under this Act may make such order as it thinks fit as to the forfeiture or disposal of any crossbow or part of a crossbow in respect of which the offence was committed.

**Explosives Act 1875**

Penalty for sale of gunpowder to children

Gunpowder shall not be sold to any person apparently under the age of sixteen years; and any person selling gunpowder in contravention of this section shall be guilty of an offence and liable on summary conviction to a fine not exceeding level 5 on the standard scale.

**Firearms Act 1968**

**22**       **Acquisition and possession of firearms by minors[5].**

(1)       It is an offence—
(a)for a person under the age of eighteen to purchase or hire an air weapon or ammunition for an air weapon;
(b)for a person under the age of eighteen to purchase or hire a firearm or ammunition of any other description.

(1A)      Where a person under the age of eighteen is entitled, as the holder of a certificate under this Act, to have a firearm in his possession, it is an offence for that person to use that firearm for a purpose not authorised by the European weapons directive.

(2)       It is an offence for a person under the age of fourteen to have in his possession any firearm or ammunition to which section 1 of this Act or section 15 of the Firearms (Amendment) Act 1988 applies, except in circumstances where under section 11(1), (3) or (4) of this Act he is entitled to have possession of it without holding a firearm certificate.

---

[5] Amended by the Violent Crime Reduction Act 2006

(3)     It is an offence for a person under the age of fifteen to have with him an assembled shot gun except while under the supervision of a person of or over the age of twenty-one, or while the shot gun is so covered with a securely fastened gun cover that it cannot be fired.

(4)     Subject to section 23 below, it is an offence for a person under the age of eighteen to have with him an air weapon or ammunition for an air weapon.

## 23    Exceptions from s. 22(4).

(1)     It is not an offence under section 22(4) of this Act for a person to have with him an air weapon or ammunition while he is under the supervision of a person of or over the age of twenty-one; but where a person has with him an air weapon on any premises in circumstances where he would be prohibited from having it with him but for this subsection, it is an offence for the person under whose supervision he is to allow him to use it for firing any missile beyond those premises.

(1A)    In proceedings against a person for an offence under subsection (1) it shall be a defence for him to show that the only premises into or across which the missile was fired were premises the occupier of which had consented to the firing of the missile (whether specifically or by way of a general consent).

(2)     It is not an offence under section 22(4)of this Act for a person to have with him an air weapon or ammunition at a time when—
(a)being a member of a rifle club or miniature rifle club for the time being approved by the Secretary of State for the purposes of this section or section 15 of the Firearms (Amendment) Act 1988, he is engaged as such a member in connection with target shooting; or
(b)he is using the weapon or ammunition at a shooting gallery where the only firearms used are either air weapons or miniature rifles not exceeding ·23 inch calibre.

(3)     It is not an offence under section 22(4) of this Act for a person of or over the age of fourteen to have with him an air weapon or ammunition on private premises with the consent of the occupier

## 24    Supplying firearms to minors.

(1)     It is an offence—
(a)to sell or let on hire an air weapon or ammunition for an air weapon to a person under the age of eighteen;
(b)to sell or let on hire a firearm or ammunition of any other description to a person under the age of eighteen.

(2)     It is an offence—
(a)to make a gift of or lend any firearm or ammunition to which section 1 of

this Act applies to a person under the age of fourteen; or

(b)to part with the possession of any such firearm or ammunition to a person under that age, except in circumstances where that person is entitled under section 11(1), (3) or (4) of this Act or section 15 of the Firearms (Amendment) Act 1988 to have possession thereof without holding a firearm certificate.

(3)     It is an offence to make a gift of a shot gun or ammunition for a shot gun to a person under the age of fifteen.

(4)     It is an offence—

(a)to make a gift of an air weapon or ammunition for an air weapon to a person under the age of eighteen ; or

(b)to part with the possession of an air weapon or ammunition for an air weapon to a person under the age of eighteen except where by virtue of section 23 of this Act the person is not prohibited from having it with him.

(5)     In proceedings for an offence under any provision of this section it is a defence to prove that the person charged with the offence believed the other person to be of or over the age mentioned in that provision and had reasonable ground for the belief.

**24A     Supplying imitation firearms to minors.**

(1)     It is an offence for a person under the age of eighteen to purchase an imitation firearm.

(2)     It is an offence to sell an imitation firearm to a person under the age of eighteen.

(3)     In proceedings for an offence under subsection (2) it is a defence to show that the person charged with the offence—

(a)believed the other person to be aged eighteen or over; and

(b)had reasonable ground for that belief.

(4)     For the purposes of this section a person shall be taken to have shown the matters specified in subsection (3) if—

(a)sufficient evidence of those matters is adduced to raise an issue with respect to them; and

(b)the contrary is not proved beyond a reasonable doubt.

**Gambling Act 2005**

**Part 4     Protection of children and young persons**

Interpretation

**45     Meaning of "child" and "young person"**

(1)     In this Act "child" means an individual who is less than 16 years old.

(2)     In this Act "young person" means an individual who is not a child but who is less than 18 years old.

Principal offences

## 46     Invitation to gamble

(1)     A person commits an offence if he invites, causes or permits a child or young person to gamble.

(2)     But subsection (1) does not apply in relation to—
(a)participation in private or non-commercial gaming,
(b)participation in private or non-commercial betting,
(c)participation in a lottery,
(d)participation in football pools,
(e)the use of a Category D gaming machine,
(f)participation in equal chance gaming in accordance with a prize gaming permit,
(g)participation in equal chance gaming at a licensed family entertainment centre,
(h)participation in prize gaming at a non-licensed family entertainment centre, or
(i)participation in prize gaming at a travelling fair in accordance with section 292.

(3)     In subsection (1) a reference to inviting a child or young person to gamble includes, in particular, a reference to intentionally—
(a)sending to a child or young person any document which advertises gambling, or
(b)bringing to the attention of a child or young person information about gambling with a view to encouraging the child or young person to gamble.

(4)     If a document which is sent to a child or young person and which advertises gambling gives the name or contact details of a person to whom payment may be made or from whom information may be obtained, that person shall be treated as having committed the offence under subsection (1) unless he proves that the document was sent—
(a)without his consent, and
(b)without his authority.

(5)     If information about gambling is brought to the attention of a child or young person and includes the name or contact details of a person to whom payment may be made or from whom information may be obtained, that person ("the advertiser") shall be treated as having committed the offence under subsection (1) unless he proves that the information was brought to the attention of the child or young person—

(a)without the advertiser's consent or authority, or

(b)as an incident of the information being brought to the attention of adults and without a view to encouraging the child or young person to gamble.

(6)    In subsections (4) and (5) "contact details" means—

(a)an address or other location,

(b)a telephone number,

(c)an internet site, or

(d)an email address.

## 47   Invitation to enter premises

(1)    A person commits an offence if he invites or permits a child or young person to enter premises if—

(a)a casino premises licence has effect in respect of the premises, and

(b)the premises are being used in reliance on that licence when the child or young person is invited or permitted to enter.

(2)    But subsection (1) does not apply where—

(a)a child or young person is permitted to enter a part of premises which are being used for a regional casino, and

(b)that part is not being used for the provision of facilities for gambling when the child or young person is permitted to enter.

(3)    The Secretary of State may for the purposes of subsection (2) by regulations make provision for—

(a)distinguishing between one part of premises and another;

(b)determining when use is being made of a part of premises.

(4)    A person commits an offence if he invites or permits a child or young person to enter premises other than a track if—

(a)a betting premises licence has effect in respect of the premises, and

(b)the premises are being used in reliance on that licence when the child or young person is invited or permitted to enter.

(5)    A person commits an offence if he invites or permits a child or young person to enter premises if—

(a)an adult gaming centre premises licence has effect in respect of the premises, and

(b)the premises are being used in reliance on that licence when the child or young person is invited or permitted to enter.

(6)    A person commits an offence if he invites or permits a child or young person to enter an area from which children and young persons are required to be excluded by virtue of section 182.

(7)    A person commits an offence if he invites or permits a child or young person to enter part of premises if—

(a)the premises are a licensed family entertainment centre,

(b)a person entering that part of the premises has access to a Category C gaming machine, and

(c)at the time when the child or young person is permitted or invited to enter, a Category C gaming machine is being used or is available for use.

## 48 Gambling

(1) A young person commits an offence if he gambles.

(2) But subsection (1) does not apply to—

(a)participation in private or non-commercial gaming,

(b)participation in private or non-commercial betting,

(c)participation in a lottery,

(d)participation in football pools,

(e)the use of a Category D gaming machine,

(f)participation in equal chance gaming in accordance with a prize gaming permit,

(g)participation in equal chance gaming at a licensed family entertainment centre,

(h)participation in prize gaming at a non-licensed family entertainment centre, or

(i)participation in prize gaming at a travelling fair in accordance with section 292.

## 49 Entering premises

A young person commits an offence if he enters premises in circumstances where a person would commit an offence under section 47 if he invited or permitted the young person to enter.

## 50 Provision of facilities for gambling

(1) A young person commits an offence if he provides facilities for gambling.

(2) But subsection (1) does not apply to the provision of facilities in connection with—

(a)private or non-commercial gaming,

(b)private or non-commercial betting,

(c)a lottery,

(d)football pools, or

(e)prize gaming at a travelling fair in accordance with section 292.

**Miscellaneous offences**

**56      Invitation to participate in lottery**

(1)      A person commits an offence if he invites, causes or permits a child to participate in a lottery other than—

(a)an incidental non-commercial lottery that is exempt for the purposes of section 258 by virtue of Part 1 of Schedule 11,

(b)a private lottery (whether a private society lottery, a work lottery or a residents' lottery) that is exempt for the purposes of section 258 by virtue of Part 2 of Schedule 11, or

(c)a lottery which forms part of the National Lottery.

(2)      Subsections (3) to (6) of section 46 shall have effect in relation to subsection (1) of this section as they have effect in relation to subsection (1) of that section; and for that purpose—

(a)references to a child or young person shall be treated as references only to a child, and

(b)references to gambling shall be treated as references to participation in a lottery.

**57      Invitation to participate in football pools**

(1)      A person commits an offence if he invites, causes or permits a child to participate in football pools.

(2)      Subsections (3) to (6) of section 46 shall have effect in relation to subsection (1) of this section as they have effect in relation to subsection (1) of that section; and for that purpose—

(a)references to a child or young person shall be treated as references only to a child, and

(b)references to gambling shall be treated as references to participation in football pools.

**58      Return of stake**

A person commits an offence if without reasonable excuse he fails to comply with a condition attached to an operating licence by virtue of section 83.

**59      Age limit for Category D gaming machines**

(1)      The Secretary of State may by order create an offence of inviting, causing or permitting a child or young person below a specified age to use a Category D gaming machine.

(2)    An order under subsection (1) may, in particular—

(a)apply (with modifications) or include provision similar to section 46(3) to (6);

(b)make consequential amendments of this Act.

(3)    Before making an order under subsection (1) the Secretary of State shall consult—

(a)the Commission,

(b)one or more persons who appear to the Secretary of State to represent the interests of persons carrying on gambling businesses, and

(c)one or more persons who appear to the Secretary of State to have knowledge about social problems relating to gambling.

(4)    An order under subsection (1) may apply to a class of Category D gaming machine determined by reference to—

(a)the nature of the facilities for gambling which are made available on the machine,

(b)the nature or value of a prize offered by the machine,

(c)the manner in which the machine operates, or

(d)any other matter.

## 62    Penalty

(1)    A person guilty of an offence under this Part shall be liable on summary conviction to—

(a)imprisonment for a term not exceeding 51 weeks,

(b)a fine not exceeding level 5 on the standard scale, or

(c)both.

(2)    But in relation to an offence committed by a young person subsection (1) shall have effect as if—

(a)paragraphs (a) and (c) were omitted, and

(b)in paragraph (b) the reference to level 5 were a reference to level 3.

(3)    In the application of subsection (1) to Scotland the reference to 51 weeks shall have effect as a reference to six months.

## 63    Reasonable belief about person's age

(1)    Where a person is charged with an offence under this Part of doing anything in relation to an individual who is a child it is a defence for the person charged to prove that—

(a)he took all reasonable steps to determine the individual's age, and

(b)he reasonably believed that the individual was not a child.

(2)    Where a person is charged with an offence under this Part of doing anything in relation to an individual who is a young person it is a defence for the person charged to prove that—

(a)he took all reasonable steps to determine the individual's age, and

(b)he reasonably believed that the individual was not a young person.

## 64      Use of children in enforcement operations

(1)     Nothing in this Part renders unlawful—

(a)anything done, in the performance of his functions, by a constable, an enforcement officer or an authorised person, or

(b)anything done by a child or young person at the request of a constable, enforcement officer or authorised person acting in the performance of his functions.

(2)     Subsection (1) applies to an order under section 59 as to the provisions of this Part.

## Intoxicating Substances (Supply) Act 1985

## 1       Offence of supply of intoxicating substance.

(1)     It is an offence for a person to supply or offer to supply a substance other than a controlled drug—

(a)to a person under the age of eighteen whom he knows, or has reasonable cause to believe, to be under that age; or

(b)to a person—

(i)who is acting on behalf of a person under that age; and

(ii)whom he knows, or has reasonable cause to believe, to be so acting,

if he knows or has reasonable cause to believe that the substance is, or its fumes are, likely to be inhaled by the person under the age of eighteen for the purpose of causing intoxication.

(2)     In proceedings against any person for an offence under subsection (1) above it is a defence for him to show that at the time he made the supply or offer he was under the age of eighteen and was acting otherwise than in the course or furtherance of a business.

(3)     A person guilty of an offence under this section shall be liable on summary conviction to imprisonment for a term not exceeding six months or to a fine not exceeding level 5 on the standard scale, or to both.

(4)     In this section "controlled drug" has the same meaning as in the Misuse of Drugs Act 1971.

## Hypnotism Act 1952

3       Prohibition on hypnotising persons under 18

A person who gives an exhibition, demonstration or performance of hypnotism on a person who has not attained the age of eighteen years at or in connection with an entertainment to which the public are admitted, whether on payment or otherwise, shall, unless he had reasonable cause to believe that that person had attained that age, be liable on summary conviction to a fine not exceeding level 3 on the standard scale.

**Licensing Act 2003**

**145      Unaccompanied children prohibited from certain premises**

(1)      A person to whom subsection (3) applies commits an offence if
(a)knowing that relevant premises are within subsection (4), he allows an unaccompanied child to be on the premises at a time when they are open for the purposes of being used for the supply of alcohol for consumption there, or
(b)he allows an unaccompanied child to be on relevant premises at a time between the hours of midnight and 5 a.m. when the premises are open for the purposes of being used for the supply of alcohol for consumption there.

(2)      For the purposes of this section
(a) "child" means an individual aged under 16,
(b)a child is unaccompanied if he is not in the company of an individual aged 18 or over.

(3)      This subsection applies
(a)to any person who works at the premises in a capacity, whether paid or unpaid, which authorises him to request the unaccompanied child to leave the premises,
(b)in the case of licensed premises, to
(i)the holder of a premises licence in respect of the premises, and
(ii)the designated premises supervisor (if any) under such a licence,
(c)in the case of premises in respect of which a club premises certificate has effect, to any member or officer of the club which holds the certificate who is present on the premises in a capacity which enables him to make such a request, and
(d)in the case of premises which may be used for a permitted temporary activity by virtue of Part 5, to the premises user in relation to the temporary event notice in question.

(4)      Relevant premises are within this subsection if
(a)they are exclusively or primarily used for the supply of alcohol for consumption on the premises, or
(b)they are open for the purposes of being used for the supply of alcohol for consumption on the premises by virtue of Part 5 (permitted temporary activities) and, at the time the temporary event notice in question has effect,

they are exclusively or primarily used for such supplies.

(5)     No offence is committed under this section if the unaccompanied child is on the premises solely for the purpose of passing to or from some other place to or from which there is no other convenient means of access or egress.

(6)     Where a person is charged with an offence under this section by reason of his own conduct it is a defence that
(a)he believed that the unaccompanied child was aged 16 or over or that an individual accompanying him was aged 18 or over, and
(b)either
(i)he had taken all reasonable steps to establish the individual's age, or
(ii)nobody could reasonably have suspected from the individual's appearance that he was aged under 16 or, as the case may be, under 18.

(7)     For the purposes of subsection (6), a person is treated as having taken all reasonable steps to establish an individual's age if
(a)he asked the individual for evidence of his age, and
(b)the evidence would have convinced a reasonable person.

(8)     Where a person ("the accused"  ) is charged with an offence under this section by reason of the act or default of some other person, it is a defence that the accused exercised all due diligence to avoid committing it.

(9)     A person guilty of an offence under this section is liable on summary conviction to a fine not exceeding level 3 on the standard scale.

(10)    In this section "supply of alcohol"  means
(a)the sale by retail of alcohol, or
(b)the supply of alcohol by or on behalf of a club to, or to the order of, a member of the club.

## 146    Sale of alcohol to children

(1)     A person commits an offence if he sells alcohol to an individual aged under 18.

(2)     A club commits an offence if alcohol is supplied by it or on its behalf
(a)to, or to the order of, a member of the club who is aged under 18, or
(b)to the order of a member of the club, to an individual who is aged under 18.

(3)     A person commits an offence if he supplies alcohol on behalf of a club
(a)to, or to the order of, a member of the club who is aged under 18, or
(b)to the order of a member of the club, to an individual who is aged under 18.

(4)     Where a person is charged with an offence under this section by reason of his own conduct it is a defence that
(a)he believed that the individual was aged 18 or over, and
(b)either
(i)he had taken all reasonable steps to establish the individual's age, or
(ii)nobody could reasonably have suspected from the individual's appearance that he was aged under 18.

(5) For the purposes of subsection (4), a person is treated as having taken all reasonable steps to establish an individual's age if
(a)he asked the individual for evidence of his age, and
(b)the evidence would have convinced a reasonable person.

(6) Where a person ("the accused" ) is charged with an offence under this section by reason of the act or default of some other person, it is a defence that the accused exercised all due diligence to avoid committing it.

(7) A person guilty of an offence under this section is liable on summary conviction to a fine not exceeding level 5 on the standard scale.

## 147 Allowing the sale of alcohol to children

(1) A person to whom subsection (2) applies commits an offence if he knowingly allows the sale of alcohol on relevant premises to an individual aged under 18.

(2) This subsection applies to a person who works at the premises in a capacity, whether paid or unpaid, which authorises him to prevent the sale.

(3) A person to whom subsection (4) applies commits an offence if he knowingly allows alcohol to be supplied on relevant premises by or on behalf of a club
(a)to or to the order of a member of the club who is aged under 18, or
(b)to the order of a member of the club, to an individual who is aged under 18.

(4) This subsection applies to
(a)a person who works on the premises in a capacity, whether paid or unpaid, which authorises him to prevent the supply, and
(b)any member or officer of the club who at the time of the supply is present on the relevant premises in a capacity which enables him to prevent it.

(5) A person guilty of an offence under this section is liable on summary conviction to a fine not exceeding level 5 on the standard scale.

## 147A Persistently selling alcohol to children

(1) A person is guilty of an offence if
(a)on 2 or more different occasions within a period of 3 consecutive months alcohol is unlawfully sold on the same premises to an individual aged under 18;
(b)at the time of each sale the premises were either licensed premises or premises authorised to be used for a permitted temporary activity by virtue of Part 5; and
(c)that person was a responsible person in relation to the premises at each such time.

(2) For the purposes of this section alcohol sold to an individual aged under 18 is unlawfully sold to him if
(a)the person making the sale believed the individual to be aged under 18; or
(b)that person did not have reasonable grounds for believing the individual to

be aged 18 or over.

(3)    For the purposes of subsection (2) a person has reasonable grounds for believing an individual to be aged 18 or over only if
(a)he asked the individual for evidence of his age and that individual produced evidence that would have convinced a reasonable person; or
(b)nobody could reasonably have suspected from the individual's appearance that he was aged under 18.

(4)    A person is, in relation to premises and a time, a responsible person for the purposes of subsection (1) if, at that time, he is
(a)the person or one of the persons holding a premises licence in respect of the premises; or
(b)the person or one of the persons who is the premises user in respect of a temporary event notice by reference to which the premises are authorised to be used for a permitted temporary activity by virtue of Part 5.

(5)    The individual to whom the sales mentioned in subsection (1) are made may, but need not be, the same in each case.

(6)    The same sale may not be counted in respect of different offences for the purpose
(a)of enabling the same person to be convicted of more than one offence under this section; or
(b)of enabling the same person to be convicted of both an offence under this section and an offence under section 146 or 147.

(7)    In determining whether an offence under this section has been committed, the following shall be admissible as evidence that there has been an unlawful sale of alcohol to an individual aged under 18 on any premises on any occasion
(a)the conviction of a person for an offence under section 146 in respect of a sale to that individual on those premises on that occasion;
(b)the giving to a person of a caution (within the meaning of Part 5 of the Police Act 1997) in respect of such an offence; or
(c)the payment by a person of a fixed penalty under Part 1 of the Criminal Justice and Police Act 2001 in respect of such a sale.

(8)    A person guilty of an offence under this section shall be liable, on summary conviction, to a fine not exceeding £10,000.

(9)    The Secretary of State may by order amend subsection (8) to increase the maximum fine for the time being specified in that subsection.

## 147B    Order suspending a licence in respect of offence under section 147A

(1)    Where the holder of a premises licence is convicted of an offence under section 147A in respect of sales on the premises to which the licence relates, the court may order that so much of the licence as authorises the sale by retail of alcohol on those premises is suspended for a period not exceeding three months.

(2)     Where more than one person is liable for an offence under section 147A relating to the same sales, no more than one order under subsection (1) may be made in relation to the premises in question in respect of convictions by reference to those sales.

(3)     Subject to subsections (4) and (5), an order under subsection (1) comes into force at the time specified by the court that makes it.

(4)     Where a magistrates' court makes an order under subsection (1), it may suspend its coming into force pending an appeal.

(5)     Section 130 (powers of appellate court to suspend section 129 order) applies (with the omission of subsection (9)) where an order under subsection (1) is made on conviction of an offence under section 147A as it applies where an order under section 129 is made on conviction of a relevant offence in Part 6.

### 149     Purchase of alcohol by or on behalf of children

(1)     An individual aged under 18 commits an offence if
(a)he buys or attempts to buy alcohol, or
(b)where he is a member of a club
(i)alcohol is supplied to him or to his order by or on behalf of the club, as a result of some act or default of his, or
(ii)he attempts to have alcohol supplied to him or to his order by or on behalf of the club.

(2)     But subsection (1) does not apply where the individual buys or attempts to buy the alcohol at the request of
(a)a constable, or
(b)a weights and measures inspector, who is acting in the course of his duty.

(3)     A person commits an offence if
(a)he buys or attempts to buy alcohol on behalf of an individual aged under 18, or
(b)where he is a member of a club, on behalf of an individual aged under 18 he
(i)makes arrangements whereby alcohol is supplied to him or to his order by or on behalf of the club, or
(ii)attempts to make such arrangements.

(4)     A person ("the relevant person" ) commits an offence if
(a)he buys or attempts to buy alcohol for consumption on relevant premises by an individual aged under 18, or
(b)where he is a member of a club
(i)by some act or default of his, alcohol is supplied to him, or to his order, by or on behalf of the club for consumption on relevant premises by an individual aged under 18, or
(ii)he attempts to have alcohol so supplied for such consumption.

(5)     But subsection (4) does not apply where
(a)the relevant person is aged 18 or over,

(b)the individual is aged 16 or 17,

(c)the alcohol is beer, wine or cider,

(d)its purchase or supply is for consumption at a table meal on relevant premises, and

(e)the individual is accompanied at the meal by an individual aged 18 or over.

(6)    Where a person is charged with an offence under subsection (3) or (4) it is a defence that he had no reason to suspect that the individual was aged under 18.

(7)    A person guilty of an offence under this section is liable on summary conviction

(a)in the case of an offence under subsection (1), to a fine not exceeding level 3 on the standard scale, and

(b)in the case of an offence under subsection (3) or (4), to a fine not exceeding level 5 on the standard scale.

## 150    Consumption of alcohol by children

(1)    An individual aged under 18 commits an offence if he knowingly consumes alcohol on relevant premises.

(2)    A person to whom subsection (3) applies commits an offence if he knowingly allows the consumption of alcohol on relevant premises by an individual aged under 18.

(3)    This subsection applies

(a)to a person who works at the premises in a capacity, whether paid or unpaid, which authorises him to prevent the consumption, and

(b)where the alcohol was supplied by a club to or to the order of a member of the club, to any member or officer of the club who is present at the premises at the time of the consumption in a capacity which enables him to prevent it.

(4)    Subsections (1) and (2) do not apply where

(a)the individual is aged 16 or 17,

(b)the alcohol is beer, wine or cider,

(c)its consumption is at a table meal on relevant premises, and

(d)the individual is accompanied at the meal by an individual aged 18 or over.

(5)    A person guilty of an offence under this section is liable on summary conviction

(a)in the case of an offence under subsection (1), to a fine not exceeding level 3 on the standard scale, and

(b)in the case of an offence under subsection (2), to a fine not exceeding level 5 on the standard scale.

## 151    Delivering alcohol to children

(1)    A person who works on relevant premises in any capacity, whether paid or unpaid, commits an offence if he knowingly delivers to an individual aged under 18

(a)alcohol sold on the premises, or

(b)alcohol supplied on the premises by or on behalf of a club to or to the order of a member of the club.

(2)     A person to whom subsection (3) applies commits an offence if he knowingly allows anybody else to deliver to an individual aged under 18 alcohol sold on relevant premises.

(3)     This subsection applies to a person who works on the premises in a capacity, whether paid or unpaid, which authorises him to prevent the delivery of the alcohol.

(4)     A person to whom subsection (5) applies commits an offence if he knowingly allows anybody else to deliver to an individual aged under 18 alcohol supplied on relevant premises by or on behalf of a club to or to the order of a member of the club.

(5)     This subsection applies
(a)to a person who works on the premises in a capacity, whether paid or unpaid, which authorises him to prevent the supply, and
(b)to any member or officer of the club who at the time of the supply in question is present on the premises in a capacity which enables him to prevent the supply.

(6)     Subsections (1), (2) and (4) do not apply where
(a)the alcohol is delivered at a place where the buyer or, as the case may be, person supplied lives or works, or
(b)the individual aged under 18 works on the relevant premises in a capacity, whether paid or unpaid, which involves the delivery of alcohol, or
(c)the alcohol is sold or supplied for consumption on the relevant premises.

(7)     A person guilty of an offence under this section is liable on summary conviction to a fine not exceeding level 5 on the standard scale.

## 152     Sending a child to obtain alcohol

(1)     A person commits an offence if he knowingly sends an individual aged under 18 to obtain
(a)alcohol sold or to be sold on relevant premises for consumption off the premises, or
(b)alcohol supplied or to be supplied by or on behalf of a club to or to the order of a member of the club for such consumption.

(2)     For the purposes of this section, it is immaterial whether the individual aged under 18 is sent to obtain the alcohol from the relevant premises or from other premises from which it is delivered in pursuance of the sale or supply.

(3)     Subsection (1) does not apply where the individual aged under 18 works on the relevant premises in a capacity, whether paid or unpaid, which involves the delivery of alcohol.

(4)     Subsection (1) also does not apply where the individual aged under 18 is sent by
(a)a constable, or
(b)a weights and measures inspector,
who is acting in the course of his duty.

(5)     A person guilty of an offence under this section is liable on summary conviction to a fine not exceeding level 5 on the standard scale.

## 153   Prohibition of unsupervised sales by children

(1)     A responsible person commits an offence if on any relevant premises he knowingly allows an individual aged under 18 to make on the premises
(a)any sale of alcohol, or
(b)any supply of alcohol by or on behalf of a club to or to the order of a member of the club, unless the sale or supply has been specifically approved by that or another responsible person.

(2)     But subsection (1) does not apply where
(a)the alcohol is sold or supplied for consumption with a table meal,
(b)it is sold or supplied in premises which are being used for the service of table meals (or in a part of any premises which is being so used), and
(c)the premises are (or the part is) not used for the sale or supply of alcohol otherwise than to persons having table meals there and for consumption by such a person as an ancillary to his meal.

(3)     A person guilty of an offence under this section is liable on summary conviction to a fine not exceeding level 1 on the standard scale.

(4)     In this section "responsible person" means
(a)in relation to licensed premises
(i)the holder of a premises licence in respect of the premises,
(ii)the designated premises supervisor (if any) under such a licence, or
(iii)any individual aged 18 or over who is authorised for the purposes of this section by such a holder or supervisor,
(b)in relation to premises in respect of which there is in force a club premises certificate, any member or officer of the club present on the premises in a capacity which enables him to prevent the supply in question, and
(c)in relation to premises which may be used for a permitted temporary activity by virtue of Part 5
(i)the premises user, or
(ii)any individual aged 18 or over who is authorised for the purposes of this section by the premises user.

154      **Enforcement role for weights and measures authorities**

(1)      It is the duty of every local weights and measures authority in England and Wales to enforce within its area the provisions of sections 146 and 147, so far as they apply to sales of alcohol made on or from premises to which the public have access.

(2)      A weights and measures inspector may make, or authorise any person to make on his behalf, such purchases of goods as appear expedient for the purpose of determining whether those provisions are being complied with.

**National Lottery Act 1993**

13      **Contravention of regulations an offence.**

(1)      If any requirement or restriction imposed by regulations made under section 12 is contravened in relation to the promotion of a lottery that forms part of the National Lottery—
(a)the promoter of the lottery shall be guilty of an offence, except if the contravention occurred without the consent or connivance of the promoter and the promoter exercised all due diligence to prevent such a contravention,
(b)any director, manager, secretary or other similar officer of the promoter, or any person purporting to act in such a capacity, shall be guilty of an offence if he consented to or connived at the contravention or if the contravention was attributable to any neglect on his part, and
(c)any other person who was party to the contravention shall be guilty of an offence.

(2)      A person guilty of an offence under this section shall be liable—
(a)on summary conviction, to a fine not exceeding the statutory maximum;
(b)on conviction on indictment, to imprisonment for a term not exceeding two years, to a fine or to both.

(3)      Summary proceedings in Scotland for an offence under this section may be commenced within a period of six months from the date on which evidence sufficient in the opinion of the procurator fiscal to warrant proceedings came to his knowledge; but no proceedings in Scotland shall be commenced by virtue of this section more than three years after the commission of the offence.

(4)      For the purposes of this section, a certificate signed by or on behalf of the procurator fiscal and stating the date on which evidence sufficient in his opinion to warrant the proceedings came to his knowledge shall be conclusive evidence of that fact; and a certificate stating that matter and purporting to be so signed shall be taken to be so signed unless the contrary is proved.

**National Lottery Regulations 1994**

3.        No National Lottery ticket shall be sold by or to a person who has not attained the age of 16 years.

**12        Petroleum (Consolidation) Regulations 2014**

(2)        No person under the age of sixteen years is to operate a dispenser on dispensing premises.

(3)        No person is to supply, or allow the supply of, petrol to a person under the age of sixteen years

**Pyrotechnic Articles (Safety) Regulations 2010**

Prohibition on supply of category 1, 2 or 3 fireworks

Regulation 15.—(1) No person shall supply—

(a)        a Christmas cracker to any person under the age of twelve years;

(b)        any other category 1 firework to any person under the age of sixteen years.

(2)        No person shall supply a category 2 or 3 firework to any person under the age of eighteen years.

(3)        In this Regulation—

"Christmas cracker" means a paper or foil tube, crimped at each end, enclosing novelties and with one or more snaps running along the length of the tube; and

"snap" means two overlapping strips of cardboard or paper, or two strings, with a friction-sensitive pyrotechnic composition in sliding contact with an abrasive surface and designed to be held in the hand."

Prohibition on supply of pyrotechnic articles

Regulation 33.—(1) No person shall supply a category 4 firework, a category T2 theatrical pyrotechnic article or a category P2 other pyrotechnic article, except to a person with specialist knowledge falling within regulation 42.

(2)        No person shall supply a category T1 theatrical pyrotechnic article or a category P1 other pyrotechnic article to a person under the age of eighteen years.

**Sunbeds (Regulation) Act 2010**

1        Main interpretative provisions.

(1)     The following provisions apply for the interpretation of this Act.

(2)     "Sunbed" means an electrically-powered device designed to produce tanning of the human skin by the emission of ultra-violet radiation.

(3)     A "sunbed business" is a business that involves making one or more sunbeds available for use on premises that are occupied by, or are to any extent under the management or control of, the person who carries on the business; and those sunbeds are the sunbeds to which the business relates.

2       Duty to prevent sunbed use by children

(1)     A person who carries on a sunbed business ("P") must secure—
(a)that no person aged under 18 uses on relevant premises a sunbed to which the business relates;
(b)that no offer is made by P or on P's behalf to make a sunbed to which the business relates available for use on relevant premises by a person aged under 18;
(c)that no person aged under 18 is at any time present, otherwise than in the course of providing services to P for the purposes of the business, in a restricted zone.

(2)     In this section "relevant premises" means premises which—
(a)are occupied by P or are to any extent under P's management or control, and
(b)are not domestic premises.

(3)     Subsections (4) and (5) have effect for determining what is for the purposes of subsection (1)(c) a "restricted zone".

(4)     If a sunbed to which the business relates is in a wholly or partly enclosed space on relevant premises that is reserved for users of that sunbed, every part of that space is a restricted zone.

(5)     If a sunbed to which the business relates is in a room on relevant premises, but not in a space falling within subsection (4), every part of that room is a restricted zone.

(6)     If P fails to comply with subsection (1), P commits an offence and is liable on summary conviction to a fine not exceeding £20,000.

(7)     It is a defence for a person ("D") charged with an offence under this section to show that D took all reasonable precautions and exercised all due diligence to avoid committing it.

(8)     This section is subject to section 3 (exemption for medical treatment).

3       Exemption for medical treatment.

(1)     The use of a sunbed falls within this subsection if—
(a)the use is for the purpose of medical treatment provided under the supervision or direction of a registered medical practitioner, and
(b)the sunbed is a dedicated sunbed in, or provided by, a healthcare establishment.

(2)      Section 2(1)(a) does not apply to any use of a sunbed that falls within subsection (1).

(3)      Section 2(1)(b) does not apply to an offer to make a sunbed available for use in a case where the use of the sunbed would fall within subsection (1).

(4)      Section 2(1)(c) does not apply in a case where a person is present in a restricted zone for the purpose of any use of a sunbed in that zone that would fall within subsection (1).

(5)      In subsection (1)—

"dedicated sunbed" means a sunbed that is made available only for use for the purpose of medical treatment;

"healthcare establishment" means—

(a) in England, a hospital as defined by section 275 of the National Health Service Act 2006;

(b) in Wales, a hospital as defined by section 206 of the National Health Service (Wales) Act 2006 or an independent hospital, independent clinic, or independent medical agency within the meaning of the Care Standards Act 2000.


4        Power to make further provision restricting use, sale or hire of sunbeds.

(1)      Regulations may make provision requiring a person who carries on a sunbed business ("P") to secure that—

(a)the use of sunbeds to which the business relates is supervised in such manner as the regulations may require;

(b)no sunbed to which the business relates is used on domestic premises by a person aged under 18;

(c)no offer is made by P or on P's behalf to make a sunbed to which the business relates available for use on domestic premises by a person aged under 18.

(2)      Regulations may make provision prohibiting or restricting the sale or hire of sunbeds to persons aged under 18.

(3)      Before making regulations under subsection (1)(a) or (2), the appropriate national authority must consult persons appearing to the appropriate national authority to have an interest in the subject-matter of the proposed regulations.

(4)      Consultation undertaken by the appropriate national authority before the commencement of this section is as effective for the purposes of subsection (3) as consultation undertaken after that time.


## Tattooing of Minors Act 1969

1        Prohibition of tattooing of minors

It shall be an offence to tattoo a person under the age of eighteen except when the tattoo is performed for medical reasons by a duly qualified medical practitioner or by a person working under his direction, but it shall be a defence for a person charged to show that at the time the tattoo was performed he had reasonable cause to believe that the person tattooed was of or over the age of eighteen and did in fact so believe.

2       Penalties

Any person committing such an offence shall be liable on summary conviction to a fine not exceeding level 3 on the standard scale, or, in the case of a second or subsequent conviction, to a fine not exceeding one level 3 on the standard scale.

**Video Recordings Act 1984** (as repealed and re-enacted by the Video Recordings Act 2010)

11      Supplying video recording of classified work in breach of classification

(1)     Where a classification certificate issued in respect of a video work states that no video recording containing that work is to be supplied to any person who has not attained the age specified in the certificate, a person who supplies or offers to supply a video recording containing that work to a person who has not attained the age so specified is guilty of an offence unless the supply is, or would if it took place be, an exempted supply.

(2)     It is a defence to a charge of committing an offence under this section to prove—
(a)that the accused neither knew nor had reasonable grounds to believe that the classification certificate contained the statement concerned,
(b)that the accused neither knew nor had reasonable grounds to believe that the person concerned had not attained that age, or
(c)that the accused believed on reasonable grounds that the supply was, or would if it took place be, an exempted supply by virtue of section 3(4) or (5) of this Act.

(3)     A person guilty of an offence under this section shall be liable, on summary conviction, to imprisonment for a term not exceeding six months or a fine not exceeding level 5 on the standard scale or both.

12      Certain video recordings only to be supplied in licensed sex shops

(1)     Where a classification certificate issued in respect of a video work states that

no video recording containing that work is to be supplied other than in a licensed sex shop, a person who at any place other than in a sex shop for which a licence is in force under the relevant enactment—

(a)supplies a video recording containing the work, or

(b)offers to do so, is guilty of an offence unless the supply is, or would if it took place be, an exempted supply.

(2)    It is a defence to a charge of committing an offence under subsection (1) above to prove—

(a)that the accused neither knew nor had reasonable grounds to believe that the classification certificate contained the statement concerned,

(b)that the accused believed on reasonable grounds that the place concerned was a sex shop for which a licence was in force under the relevant enactment, or

(c)that the accused believed on reasonable grounds that the supply was, or would if it took place be, an exempted supply by virtue of section 3(4) of this Act or subsection (6) below.

(3)    Where a classification certificate issued in respect of a video work states that no video recording containing that work is to be supplied other than in a licensed sex shop, a person who has a video recording containing the work in his possession for the purpose of supplying it at any place other than in such a sex shop is guilty of an offence, unless he has it in his possession for the purpose only of a supply which, if it took place, would be an exempted supply.

(4)    It is a defence to a charge of committing an offence under subsection (3) above to prove—

(a)that the accused neither knew nor had reasonable grounds to believe that the classification certificate contained the statement concerned,

(b)that the accused believed on reasonable grounds that the place concerned was a sex shop for which a licence was in force under the relevant enactment, or

(c)that the accused had the video recording in his possession for the purpose only of a supply which he believed on reasonable grounds would, if it took place, be an exempted supply by virtue of section 3(4) of this Act or subsection (6) below.

(4A)   A person guilty of an offence under subsection (1) or (3) above shall be liable, on summary conviction, to imprisonment for a term not exceeding six months or a fine not exceeding level 5 on the standard scale or both.

(5)    In this section "relevant enactment" means Schedule 3 to the Local Government (Miscellaneous Provisions) Act 1982 ... and "sex shop" has the same meaning as in the relevant enactment.

(6)    For the purposes of this section, where a classification certificate issued in respect of a video work states that no video recording containing that work is

to be supplied other than in a licensed sex shop, the supply of a video recording containing that work—

(a)to a person who, in the course of a business, makes video works or supplies video recordings, and

(b)with a view to its eventual supply in sex shops, being sex shops for which licences are in force under the relevant enactment, is an exempted supply.

# INDEX

Bold numbers are where a detailed explanation is provided.